For my daughters
fierce, wise and beautiful

Farflung

International Adoptees Rising
Real and Resilient

ANNE POLLACK

Farflung:

International Adoptees Rising Real and Resilient

by Anne Pollack
© 2020 Anne Pollack

Published by Endless Skies Press, Ashland, Oregon.

Book Design: Chris Molé, booksavvystudio.com

Library of Congress Control Number: 2020919316

ISBN: 978-0-578-67914-3

First Edition

Printed in the United States of America

Contents

FARFLUNG

"ALL, LIKE DIAMOND,

IS CARBON FIRST, THEN LIGHT."

— JOSE MARTI

INTRODUCTION

WHEN I FIRST BEGAN THIS PROJECT I interviewed teenage adoptees and needed to get their parents' permission to do so. Often the initial reaction from the parent was something like this: "Oh, that sounds interesting. But she/he never talks about adoption issues and I doubt very much she/he will want to be interviewed. Still, I'll ask."

And then the follow up: "I was really surprised. She/he really *does* want to talk."

If this book has caught your eye, chances are it is because you were once among the thousands of children who left birth family and country to come to a foreign land through no choice of your own. And you have a lot to say about your life experience. You know firsthand what it means to navigate your way through the issues that come with the territory of international adoption, issues that can be particularly challenging—just as they also make you uniquely interesting.

Our internationally adopted daughter became the impetus for this book project when she began grappling with some difficult questions related to her adoption. I knew she would benefit from support and encouragement beyond what we could offer and I wanted to connect her directly with the wisdom of adoptees who offer the benefit of their own experience and courage. Within the safety of the pages of a book, I hoped to gently intrude on her isolation and encourage her to explore some tough issues. And as much as we have been open to discussing everything adoption-related in our family, I knew there was no substitute for the authentic voices and perspectives of adoptees themselves. So I began the hunting and gathering process for her, speaking with many international adoptees along the way. Years later that process culminated in this book.

The "hunting and gathering" is reflected in these pages through a weave of live and researched interviews, as well as writings of adoptees. The voices of adoptees have been the primary force shaping this project with the hope of inspiring you the reader to express what is real for you, to tap into your innate wisdom and resilience. And ultimately to connect with one another.

Out of all of these first-person accounts, four main themes emerged to create the scaffolding for this book: Gratitude, belonging, racial and cultural difference, and living with contradictions. Each theme is fleshed out with comments and questions by adoptees and realized through poetry or short stories seeded with their actual words and experiences. At the end of each section you will find pages with writing prompts for journaling or sketching or whatever springs from your creative heart.

To all of those who willingly offered your time and your trust to engage in adoption conversations with me, I am deeply grateful. Sharing your stories and your willingness to sometimes enter uncertain territory in our talks has been not only a great learning experience for me but an enduring privilege. And to those whose words culled from other sources enrich these pages, you have my utmost appreciation. Each of you has put flesh on the bones of the international adoptee experience for all of us who are connected to adoption in some way.

Note: Interview segments are attributed with pseudo first names. Material from known sources appear with full names and footnoted sources.

You might wonder what would be the point of reading a book for international adoptees put together by an adoptive parent. Fair question. My answer unfolds bit by bit throughout the book. However, I begin here with what has always been my intention: To remain in the background in this project and to allow the experiences and collective wisdom of adoptees to fuel the book and occupy the foreground. I believe that the words and thoughts expressed by adoptees will resonate with you, either by echoing your own or by challenging you with new ideas to consider. I have no doubt that these adoptees will inspire you with their honesty, their spirit and resilience, qualities you will come to recognize in yourselves.

I am a Licensed Clinical Social Worker (LCSW). I have no connection with adoption agencies. My only agenda in creating this resource has been to empower and encourage adoptees to express their thoughts, feelings and questions in connection with adoption issues, to find their own resilience, and to discover the amazing uniqueness that is theirs—together with a sense of belonging to the extensive and vital international adoptee community.

I wish you well on your journeys.

The Tangle of Gratitude

GRATITUDE IS THE MOST BENEFICIAL EMOTION for the human brain. Even better than love, believe it or not. Our physical, psychological, and social well-being are all greatly enhanced by a sense of feeling grateful.

Psychology professor Robert Emmons of University of California, Davis is one of the world's leading scientific experts on the subject. He studied over a thousand people from ages eight to 80 who practiced gratitude consistently and reported the following benefits:[1]

- Stronger Immune Systems
- Longer, More Refreshing Sleep
- Greater Optimism
- Increased Alertness
- Increased Generosity and Compassion
- The Ability to Be More Forgiving
- Decrease in Feelings of Loneliness

So, what's not to like? You can't really argue with gratitude. Right?

But when it comes to being adopted, being grateful takes some unique twists and turns.

Your adoptive family probably provided you with food, clothing, shelter, love, and abundant opportunities that would not otherwise have been within reach. But the expectation, spoken or unspoken, for you to express *only* gratitude—or the possibility that gratitude might obliterate the inevitable grief imbedded in adoption, along

FARFLUNG – Anne Pollack

with the natural need to explore your feelings and history—can be a set-up for pain and confusion.

What's more, this message can create a chill on adoptee relationships with family and friends because it breeds inauthenticity.

Gratitude gets intertwined around so many things: Parents' need for approval and appreciation, your need to take care of your parents' feelings, your need for a sense of belonging to family and surrounding community. Yet anger, sadness and other strong painful emotions can and do naturally exist alongside a sense of gratitude. They are "roommates in the house of feelings"—maybe even siblings—meaning they struggle at times, vie for attention, but are basically capable of living side by side in the same dwelling.

To that end, let's first get rid of labels like "the angry adoptee" or "the grateful adoptee" or "the perfect parent." These serve no one and only cultivate misunderstanding. Everyone needs to be heard in their own voice and in their own words without lip-syncing someone else's. We need to really hear about each other's experience, not just what we would like to hear or what meshes with our preconceived ideas.

It's no surprise that so many international adoptees have lots to say about gratitude and expectations of gratitude. Let's listen to a few of them unfiltered.

ADOPTEES ON GRATITUDE

"I was also trying to understand why everyone thought I should be grateful because I was adopted. Or why they told me that my adoptive parents saved me. Or why people felt that being upset or angry is an irrational response to living, forever, with no answers."
—SHAARON PINE[2]

~

"*I was really focused on being a good kid... I was trying to earn my place in the family, to make sure they weren't sorry they adopted me. I had to go with the flow, do what was expected, not create a lot of waves, fly under the radar. This was a lot of what tamped down a desire to explore my identity. My father was a minister and he used to say to me, 'Your coming to us was a miracle from God.' I heard that as I better do something really good in return...*

"*My own mother was adopted. I remember when I was in college, learning that her birth mother had lived in the same city. 'Well, did you ever try to contact her?' 'No,' she said, 'because that would have been a slap in the face to my (adoptive) mother and I couldn't do that.' That was the singular moment of input—nothing before or after. The message I got was 'If you appreciate anything we've done for you, you will never look for your family.' I didn't feel the freedom to express anything about adoption until I was out of the house.*" —Dierdre

~

"*Frustration is the immediate word I want to go to (in reaction to the word gratitude). In many ways, I think my parents kind of screwed up, invalidated myself and my dignity. I absolutely know that my father would become defensive about that. 'How ungrateful are you?' And that's so tough. I mean on the one hand I love them, and I know I hit the jackpot. But at the end of the day, I know I didn't have a choice in that. There were a lot of things that really fucked with me growing up.*

"*I mean I've talked about this with my counselor, too. There is absolutely a world where you can feel all those things [re: gratitude] and it would be absolutely fine. But I think that would be really hard for my parents to grasp.*" —Devon

∼

"She (my mom) just let me be who I needed to be and figure it out on my own, which I really appreciate. Always reminding me how much she loves me. Even when you're being a bratty teenager and telling them how much you hate them, and they tell you how much they love you, it's those moments that make you thankful..." —MALLORY

∼

"Before I found other adoptees online I thought that my adoptive parents' constant admonitions to be grateful to them, grateful for all they had done for me, grateful for all they had sacrificed for me, grateful to them for taking me in and 'loving' me, was just part of their overall abusive parenting pattern, but I was shocked and saddened at the number of adoptees who had had the same litany all the way through their own childhoods from their own adoptive parents.

"I am not grateful to my adoptive parents for doing some of the things parents are supposed to do.

"...Gratitude is not a payment system. But somehow adoptees are supposed to be more indebted to their adoptive parents than real kids are, somehow bringing up adopted kids is more of a sacrifice than bringing up real kids, and so goddammit adopted kids should fawn all over their adopted parents in 'gratitude.'

"As adoptees it's often not just our adoptive families who expect us to be 'grateful,' who expect us to never say a bad word about our adoptive parents—who expect us to never say anything critical about adoption—the whole of society does it, and if we were lucky enough to have parents who didn't constantly demand our gratitude, we still got that message all the way through our lives. If we don't meet the expectations of gratitude we are labeled 'ungrateful,' and somehow

because we are ungrateful about adoption, about being adopted, we somehow must be bitter and unhappy about everything else in our lives. That's just ridiculous." —ANONYMOUS[3]

~

"When my adopted identity within my adoptive family exclusively indicates that I need to be grateful, and that gratefulness determines what can and cannot be important to me, I've been made out to be a little less human than everyone else.

"Very simply, no child has to be 'grateful' when their human rights are met." — AMANDA H. L. TRANSUE-WOOLSTON[4]

~

THE FLIP SIDE OF LUCKY

With one eye squeezed shut, Aruun could feel his fingernails grate against the camera. Watching the heat waves dance off a mountain of jeweled brilliance in the distance that might as well be Oz itself. Completely captured by the image before him, he missed the trembling that rippled from core to fingertips like the subtlest of shock waves. His camera tumbled out of his hands into the dust, the casualty of inattention that snapped him back into focus.

Aruun bent in slow motion to retrieve the camera, scooping it back into his hand and taking care to trap particles of dirt under his fingernails. This was, after all, the earth of his beginnings. Was he not entitled to at least a bit of it?

He rose to his feet, the fierce light glancing off the shimmering horizon drawing water from his eyes as he moved steadily forward. Being slender and not so tall, Aruun normally had a kind of weightlessness in his step. But on this day his legs were stiff, and his arms had lost their swing. Even with the temperature at 80 degrees, he was strangely chilled, his mustard colored t-shirt feeling flimsy despite its look of wildness with the black graphic of a galloping horse threatening to break free of its cotton/poly prison.

The t-shirt, a gift from his friend Cheyenne on the eve of his journey to India, was the one Aruun wore when he needed to be reminded that he was not entirely alone, even if he felt like he mostly was. It meant a lot, this gift, but he could never tell her that. He had just said "thanks" as he started a slow smile, and she had been able to fill in the rest with understanding. He was confident of that.

The air was heating up, but Aruun clutched his upper arms as if to guard against a cold that wasn't there and to steady himself from shaking. Bizarrely, a shrine appeared to be illuminated in the distance. It was here nineteen years ago where his tiny body had been discovered on the edge of this cloud of light, swaddled in a tattered gray cloth—the merest possible protection from the merciless sun. Only the slimmest shaving of luck between his infant body and starving, hollow-eyed dogs. He often wondered how he had ever dodged such a bleak fate. Yet here he was, nearly two decades later, slowly closing the distance between himself and this Delhi garbage dump—not a shrine of the usual variety.

Suddenly a wall of heat snagged and sealed him inside an oven of stench. As Aruun stumbled, he instinctively yanked the neck of his shirt up over his nose and mouth, but it was useless. The smells poured in without invitation, undeterred by a simple layer of fabric. He coughed up his breakfast and spewed it into a pile at his feet as a three-legged mottled dog lunged for it, gulping voraciously. Swiping at the vomit on his chin with the back of his hand, Aruun's eyes immobilized in their dry sockets as he pushed ahead past the dog, past the broken bottles, the betel nut wrappers, the warped cans oozing foul food, and half-empty bags of potato chips hovering on air currents.

Skeletal dogs, rag pickers hoping to find some recyclable bits to sell for a few *paises* and stray cows with bones you could count from 12 feet away—all rifling through this hell together. Bejeweled and dazzling from a distance, a tenement up close, this fifty-foot tower of foam slippers, shattered glass, and crushed aluminum saturated him with the scent of decay and discard cooking together in the heat. What looked so gleamingly magical minutes ago became an utterly different universe close at hand. The initial wonder of it all fell away in large chunks as Aruun's heart struggled to grasp all that his senses offered. This, his very first bed, was as shocking as it was somehow utterly familiar.

For an instant, Aruun's mind spun away to a far easier memory of an eighth grade Language Arts class. He had to write a paragraph describing a smell (bacon frying, his choice), homework that had taken him hours because the language just wouldn't materialize. How would he ever be able to convey *this* experience, even to those few close to him—this panorama of waste that had glistened almost glamorously with the help of distance and a yearning imagination?

The shirt with the galloping steed was a piece of pointless protection, so Aruun let it drop away from his nose. He shuddered, glued, unable to run away, helpless to do anything but stare in his great desire to embed every detail in his memory even as part of his mind refused to receive all that was before him. A rapid pulsing began again in his throat and quickly took up residence every-where—heart, stomach, behind his knees. He clenched his eyes shut against the bleaching sun, but there, stubbornly remaining in his mind's vision, was the image of the small shrouded bundle placed on the edge of this dump. Placed, as he so hoped, with regret and tenderness. Tears swarmed behind his eyelids. His fingertips pressed in, but there was no point. And he, who was never given to feeling sad for himself for much of anything, shook with years of weeping.

Aruun remained fixed to his spot for a handful of minutes—or maybe it was hundreds—before he began retreating back toward today's starting point. He had felt chilled, but his shirt was soaked, his black-rimmed glasses splattered with dust particles. As he lifted his arm to wipe his face, he felt a gentle but uncomprehending hand on his shoulder.

"Aruun?"

No words of response came from him. No new gesture from

her—but also no apparent desire on her part to see or to linger. None of this escaped him, but he gave no evidence. After all, this was his mother, the one to whom he was assigned long ago. How could he ever explain any of this to her, of all people, who had no entry point of understanding? In only a matter of seconds he collected more assumptions, including the belief that her lack of comprehension was the same as an absence of caring.

"I'm sorry but it's time to go. Ready or not. The group is waiting back at the hotel."

"Sure. Okay, mom." his voice muffled in the wind that tossed and rattled the discarded objects behind him like a taunting call.

They had begun the trek back to the car when Aruun suddenly pivoted and darted back to the dump, his thin legs pumping and his too-large t-shirt whipping behind him like a flag.

"What are you doing? We are *LATE*," his mother called over the plumes of dirt.

"Forgot the pictures. Be right back."

Corinne shifted from foot to foot, her default movement when nothing else was available. She deepened the perpetual crease between her eyebrows and adjusted her outsized sunglasses. What could she do with this son of hers, who always kept himself just out of reach? She crossed her arms over her pink sun dress, briefly considering some options for closing the distance between them before settling on the familiar idea of giving him the space he needed as he struggled and grew up—though every once in a while continuing to step in to provide an experience involving Indian food and opportunities like this homeland journey. She quietly and heartily congratulated herself for the success of the conscious parenting path she had chosen.

Aruun ran back breathing hard. He tucked the camera back into its case as Corinne reached over to brush off some of the debris still clinging to his forehead, but only succeeded in smearing dark stripes where the flecks had been. "Whoops," she said trying to lighten things by laughing at herself. Aruun swiped the stripes away with his sweaty hand. She tried once again to reach out in a way that she felt to be motherly. After all, any outsider could see that she was wholly devoted and committed. "Wanna talk?" she said, cocking her head with concern.

"Not really."

"We have a minute or two. Just tell me, how did that go?"

"I actually don't want to talk right now, if you don't mind. Or even if you do."

"Please don't be rude, Aruun. We love you very much. That's why we brought you here."

"I know, I know. That's not the issue. I appreciate your spending the cash and all. I really do."

"So what *is* the issue then?"

He looked at her sideways through the screen of his bangs. "Later, ok?"

"Suit yourself, Aruun."

They reached the edge of the site where the driver in a white van was waiting. Aruun stood before a sign, squinting in order to read it:

In Ghazipur, IL&FS has ambitious plans to build a new waste-to-energy plant that will slowly eat away the massive tower of trash. The company is seeking ways to supplement the incomes of 450 small local dairy farms with a biomass plant and to provide better housing for about 375 slum families associated with the Ghazipur flower market and other local cottage industries.

In the days before the IL&FS Project, this site was just another dumping ground. Aruun knew himself to be just one of those discarded objects. Discarded by someone. Discovered by another. But who? A child picking through rubbish to generate income in place of going to school? An old woman in slippers crouching and burning in the sun? A dog? A rat? Probably an old woman. Maybe his grandmother. Maybe money changed hands, a baby stolen and sold.

The unknown, untold story replaced the one he had been spoon-fed for his first few years, the one that was decorated with words like "destiny" and "angels." He had found comfort in this narrative for a while, until on his eighth birthday he suddenly spied the underbelly of the story: For someone to have found him, there must have first been someone who had lost him.

This abyss of unanswered questions and broken heartedness seemed endless in this moment. He wrenched his thoughts away, returned to the landscape of gratitude so familiar and carefully cultivated. In fact, he *was* grateful. At least the orphanage documents had indicated the place he had been found. That was a piece of luck. It gave him a sense of place, even if it was *this* place. And at least the orphanage was supposed to have been better than some.

He knew he should be grateful for these things. And he was. Look, he told himself, you survived, wrapped for discovery, while other babies were discarded for forgetting. You were lucky enough to have been delivered from dump to decent orphanage, then to Corinne and Brad in western Mass., so what's your problem, man?

A bitter taste collected on his tongue, slightly reminiscent of the dump stench. Aruun popped some anise seeds in his mouth and climbed into the minivan after his mother, out of habit reaching for the seatbelt that wasn't actually there. *No safety measures here,* he remembered as he leaned back and shivered against the blast of air conditioning. Well, at least he wouldn't be overheated if he flew through the windshield. (And for that he was also grateful. He actually hated being hot and sweaty.) Nonetheless, he did consider asking the driver to dial the fan down, but opted instead to zip himself inside his hoodie, swaddling his body against the cold while he sought a measure of warmth from the creeping cynicism that enveloped him.

After a long ride in chilly silence, they pulled in front of the hotel where the adoptee group and their families were standing outside—yeah, waiting, just as his mom had warned. "ArUUN" they shouted, fifteen other adoptees, mostly girls sporting English names, all bound together in this homeland journey. Not much of a paper trail history for any one of them, or even mementos. It was common practice for orphanage workers to trash the small bits of linkage that were often left with babies—a photograph, a note, a tiny bracelet on the ankle—there simply was not enough space to organize and store all these little pieces of personal history for the relentless flow of babies.

Aruun was an only child in the only family he could remember. In his first family, the original biological one, he might have been one of several, or even many. No idea. In his adoptive family, he was solitary: The only adopted child, the only son, the only Indian.

Being among adoptees in this homeland journey group had been an awakening. Like one of those alarm clocks with a soft light that keeps growing stronger, this feeling of connection that had initially been rather dim had steadily brightened over the past two weeks. A new phenomenon, he greeted it with equal parts caution and gratitude.

On this December night in Delhi, the air was moist and alive with exotic spices and exhaust fumes. Monuments of old nudged up against skyscrapers. Aruun and his new friends crammed close on the crowded sidewalks and headed out for their farewell dinner in the walled old city.

He was happy to replace his garbage dump with these companions, girls who treated him like a friend instead of a pet. This was a refreshing change from what had too often been the case from grade school all the way through high school in the small, not unsophisticated college town in western Massachusetts where he had grown up. Back home, his slight build and quiet manner seemed to be an invitation for girls to hang out without flirting and confide in him like a little brother. In truth, he was not altogether unhappy with the attention. Sometimes, he was even (secretly) grateful.

Holly, who had two inches of height on him, walked a few paces with her head on his shoulder. "I am soooooo tired," she said. "These cities are way too intense. But at least I finally got over my actual jet lag."

"Just in time for a trip home."

"Right!" she burst out with a laugh like logs popping in the fire. The sound of it always gave him a spurt of joy, and tonight he grinned into the darkness. "I'm gonna miss you and everybody" she said.

"And India?"

"Yeah, yeah, India, too. Lots to think 'n write about. So. How did your day go?"

"Oh, okay I guess. Lots of clicking and snapping."

"Really?" she said, her strong, dark eyebrows approaching each other in confusion. She lifted her head off his shoulder and looked straight ahead blankly. Aruun turned and looked at her, truly amazed.

"You know my camera is my appendage, right? You didn't miss that, I trust?"

"Oh, right, right. Sorry, I just got distracted. Hey, did you know there was a bird hospital in this temple compound?"

Okay... he rolled his eyes. And instantly forgave her. How could he not? She had this warm heart and easy, explosive laugh. Plus, there actually were a ton of distractions. How could he expect her to just focus on him? His own parents didn't, and he was their only child.

The unmarked mouth of the alley was known only to Navya, their group guide, which made this visit to a century-old restaurant intriguing even to the most jaded among them. Inside the dining room, which seated two hundred people, the din and the aromas mingled together in a haze through which the group threaded their way until they arrived at a long table reserved for them. Giant gleaming steel pots burbled with aromatic sauces next to sizzling kebabs as two men rolled dough into a ball that one pressed flat and pushed inside a tandoor oven.

Clearly there were things to be learned here: The masala spice mix was a highly secret recipe, their guide Navya had told them, closely guarded by the family uncle who disappeared upstairs each night with several wooden boxes which he filled with carefully parceled out portions of spices to be hand delivered downstairs the next day. And the half inch of oil on the top of every bowl of stew was not to be eaten, but just meant to prove that the food was cooked so well that the fat had turned to liquid that you were supposed to drain off into a separate bowl. After two weeks of cultural immersion, these homeland journeyers—Indian by birth, American by culture—were still more than a little clueless, and they knew it.

Aruun watched as the waiters paraded plate after platter past them, eventually arriving at their table. When his order landed in front of him, he could feel his salivary glands kick into gear. He surveyed the *dum pukht*: Meat, herbs, and spices sealed with dough and slow-cooked. The normal order for the group was closer to chicken curry laced with onion and tomato—no one, not even the adventurous Holly, had ordered fried brains or roasted baby goat.

He ate fast while the bubbling conversation swirled around him, voices rising and falling, intermingling melodies of mostly joking exchanges competing for the high ground in both volume and cleverness. Platters of desserts began to arrive: *Kulfi* (ice cream), *ras malai* dumplings, and crispy deep-fried *jalebi*. The warm scent of cardamom mingled with animated talk throughout the restaurant; strangers, friends, and aromas melding together.

Suddenly overwhelmed by something nameless, Aruun shoved his chair away from the table. Holly leaned over.

"What's up, my buddy? Heading for the...?"

"Nope. Just need some fresh air, and maybe some last-minute visuals."

"Fresh?!? I don't think so. Want some company?"

"Thanks. I think I need some solo time right now. Back in a few."

"Uh. Okaaay. I get it," she said. Though how could she really? *He* didn't even get it. But, still, he was glad and grateful for this new friendship that had blossomed so quickly and naturally right before his very eyes.

Aruun stopped to let his mother know what he was up to. She caught his eye briefly in the midst of some topical conversation she was having, and with an absent touch on his arm with one hand, she gave a wave with the other. He stepped through the doorway and plunged out into the night, no idea of why, what, or where, with just the unsettled drumming of his heart as the backbeat.

He found himself lurching forward into Chandni Chowk market or Moonlight Square—certain that he would find whatever lasting images he needed here to complete his journey. Dating from 1650, Chandni Chowk was once the queen of market places with a pool in the center which glimmered with moonlight. These days the pool is no more but the market is one of India's busiest. Congested, noisy and still pulsing with history.

He had been here before. Not in the "deja vu" sort of way, but in real life with the group the previous day. During that crazy 90-minute visit he had snacked, wandered, and shot plenty of pics of his friends for memories and for posting. Experienced tourists advise visiting the market once, not twice, because the magnitude of the noise, chaos, and sensory overload battered the energy reserves. And while that was totally true, he was far from finished with it. The urgency of this second immersion flooded him and compelled him to return. But this time alone.

Aruun leaned left and right, twisting and stretching to grab images quickly. He was short of breath, completely focused, and utterly distracted. Piles of brilliant orange, fuchsia, violet, and turquoise fabrics threatened to tug his eyes out of their deep-set orbs. Trays of sweets, hundreds of unknown varieties it seemed, were laid out before him, the tantalizing foreground for boxes of electronics. Aruun snapped a shot and then bought himself a jalebi fried in pure ghee. At the first bite, it broke, and stumbling to catch it he was cut off by a small boy in a red turban who was making a game out of artfully dodging the market-goers as he chased a ball. Stopping to steady himself, camera swinging from his wrist, he swiped the ghee dripping from his chin then quickly licked his camera clean.

No doubt this is what drew the eye of a wiry twenty-something man. Aruun looked up into what seemed to be some version of himself staring back—except these eyes were not neutral as he imagined his own appeared to be. They were smoldering, questioning, considering. He pointed his camera at the young man and clicked a could-have-been self-portrait of a guy clawing his way to independence in the thick of Old Delhi, where he, Aruun, seemed to belong—except that he didn't, lacking the "entry permits" afforded by language and culture.

As the young man stepped forward, Aruun braced for an angry confrontation over the captured photo. Internally, he rehearsed a gesture of apology, but that plan was quickly derailed.

"Come," the young man motioned. "We go to spice market. Many beautiful pictures take. Good price. Only 400 rupees. Comecome." And he pointed to a green rickshaw, probably the most efficient way to travel through the narrow, twisting streets choked with cars and hawkers and animals.

Aruun hestitated. There was the group convening for the farewell dinner. And his mother. With all her blank spots, she didn't deserve the worry. After all, it was her idea to bring him back to India, just as it had been her idea to bring him out of India. And he was grateful. He held up one finger to signal a pause to his would-be tour guide.

"Hi mom. It's me at 7:00. Actually 7:10. About to board a rickshaw for a quick photo trip to the spice market. Don't worry, okay? See you soon."

Satisfied that he had fulfilled his responsibility via voicemail, and barely registering that his battery was down to only nine percent, he nodded to the driver, who once again pointed to the rickshaw parked nearby and motioned for Aruun to climb in.

Something about this guy was vaguely alarming. But what was it exactly? He kind of reeked of a toxic stew of hunger and cleverness. Maybe this was just Aruun's paranoia speaking freely, as it had many times in the past.

He searched the dimly lit chambers of his mind for hard evidence of real danger, but most of what he unearthed was dread and confusion about tomorrow's departure. He settled himself awkwardly on the bench, tilting away from the gash in the vinyl.

The driver easily swung his leg over the bicycle seat and muscled the two of them into the night through the dark and unruly alleyways, snaking around like the intestines of a deer Aruun had once seen split open by the side of the road in Massachusetts.

They wheeled past masses of people haggling, smoking, gesturing incessantly. They wove in and out of the crush of small cars, motorbikes, and rickshaws. Floating through his mind was a childhood game he used to play with Curtis and Richie from down the block. They would cover each other's eyes, spinning around the blindfolded one until he became disoriented enough to do amusing and ridiculous things.

At this point in his unplanned tour, Aruun's normally reliable sense of direction had faded away. But this was no play date on the lawn of a brick house in New England. His intuition stirred as if ruffled by a slight breeze. He yanked off a hangnail and watched a bead of blood form, doing his utmost to resist the small voice that was politely requesting his attention. Venturing out with this driver was what mattered, and he would not be dissuaded.

The guide pitched his body forward in an effort to haul them through the throngs of vehicles and wandering people, but it was slow going. No one walked briskly, although they must have had destinations in mind. Aruun pulled out his crumpled map to see if he could figure out if they were closing in on the Khari Baoli, the largest wholesale spice market in Asia, but the light was too murky for navigation even though bulbs were strung through the passageways, each with its own harsh halo. Pairs of dark eyes met his everywhere and he wondered if they recognized him. "It's ME," he felt like shouting. "Take me to my family!"

The rickshaw came to a halt at the side of an alley and the driver pointed ahead to the spice market. Aruun pulled up an analog clock face on his cell to show him when he wanted to be returned to the restaurant, thirty minutes from now, and the driver nodded once to signal his comprehension. Aruun stepped out, resolve in his stride, hesitation in his heart.

And then there it was: A mountain range of spices, nuts, herbs, rice, and tea. He stood still as his eyes devoured the colors and textures, from the wrinkled bright red chilis and rusty orange turmeric to tin plates of tiny mustard seeds swelling into modest brown peaks. The scent of cardamom pulled him toward the right, where he spied the soft green powder close at hand. He longed to plunge his hands into its velvety fragrance and carry it home on his skin.

He was so grateful to be here, to have his senses bathed like this at the market. For a moment he forgot his quietly pulsing apprehension. Aruun closed his eyes briefly so he could shut out the visual and allow the aromas to envelope him. He tried to tease out each individual strand of scent—cinnamon, saffron, coriander, human sweat. The cacophony of the market and the vivid confusion of smells made him sway with dizziness. Behind his left shoulder he heard laughter, and instinctively opened his eyes and turned around. Two boys were watching him, amused. Normally, he would have smiled, at least a little. But tonight, he turned away; annoyed, feeling singled out, misunderstood, disrespected in his own land.

He walked on.

The sound of plinking reached him as a smokey flow of black cascaded into the brass bowl of a scale where they landed as individual tiny balls of peppercorns. Aruun reached for his camera and took thirteen pictures, then checked the time. Ten minutes had already passed. He spotted a stall with a burlap bag piled with saffron and bought ten threads for his mother. He knew she did not really want to leave India without them.

He turned and saw cashews split open exposing their vulnerable interiors, like offering your throat to the wolves or the inside of your arm to the nurse taking your blood. He made a portrait of the cashews, then expanded his vision to a man in a short-sleeve white shirt standing behind them who bared the inside of his veined arm as he scooped for a customer.

Actually it seemed that almost every man was wearing some sort of white shirt, including himself—but his t-shirt had small letters on the pocket that spelled out "college student," which he once thought was such a sly American joke that he had to bring it on the trip. But wearing it here felt strange, not funny or cool, and just highlighted his sense that despite his physical appearance, he did not quite fit. Like at home, where despite speaking unaccented American English, he didn't quite mesh either. In fact, his joke t-shirt was spot on: He was a generic college student, without a major. His parents telegraphed their disappointment in silence and mutely paid his junior college tuition. For which he was grateful. Of course.

Aruun hurried out of the market the exact way he had entered: Past the aromatic textured mounds, past the women in their brilliant saris, through the carved archway crisscrossed with so many cables that it looked like a prison camp. With a jerk of his head, he looked first left and then right, anxious to find his driver, although in truth he could certainly have found another.

When he finally spotted the rickshaw, he ambled over to it and climbed inside, this time sitting squarely on top of the gash in the seat. Still swathed in the images of the spice market, Aruun assumed that he would now be returned to Chandni Chowk. After all, that was their understanding, so there was no need to discuss it again. But suddenly, the driver took off without warning, forcing Aruun to bounce hard on the seat ripping the gash in the upholstery into a larger gaping hole.

Aruun's mind lurched from enticing mounds of tea leaves and pistachios to the women swirled in brilliantly colored cloth hovering over them. The smells of spices burned into his memory with the sounds of horns and endless chattering. He thought of tomorrow's departure, of the very long plane trip home with his mother as his only companion, running through what he had captured for keeps in his camera and his imagination.

Suddenly he realized that none of this was new to him: The garbage dump, the babbling in languages he didn't speak, the color-saturated scenes, and the oppressive heat that heightened their brilliance, were everything he had always known. Being in India was a shock, but it was also an ordinary reminder of what he had always carried several levels below his awareness, so far unspoken.

It had been many minutes since he had focused on the twisting roads beyond the rickshaw instead of the alleyways of his own mind. The real roads had begun to extend themselves, and as the driver picked up speed, yanking Aruun out of his reverie, he realized this could not be the way back to Chandni Chowk.

"No, no," he yelled. "I need to go back. STOP!!"

"First, we go to my cousin. Not too far."

"No, no, NO!! TURN AROUND!!" Aruun shouted, his throat pulsing with heat, his voice sucked away in the traffic.

The driver answered with a wave of his hand and continued on. The rickshaw pulled forward and Aruun began to panic. He struggled to his feet and stood up like a chariot driver while the man pumping the wheels cranked up his speed, darting in and out of traffic. Hanging on with a death grip, Aruun shouted, his voice rising in a steaming vapor. "Fuck you, dude! I said FUCK YOU! STOP THIS FUCKING CRATE!"

There was a dark form ahead in the middle of the road. As they closed in it morphed into a stray cow standing stunned, paralyzed by the honking and yelling. All vehicles converged on the animal, waiting for a chance to skirt around it. Aruun seized that moment, leaped out of the rickshaw and broke into a run. He heard the driver yell, cranking his rig around the cow in a U-turn and pedaling after him, but Aruun's panic made him nimble. He zigzagged into side alleys without stopping, although with no sense at all of where to go. Chest heaving, hoping he had finally eluded the driver, he disappeared into a doorway and was absorbed by the darkness. He peered uneasily into the faces beyond him, still short of breath, and pulled out his cellphone—only seven percent charge left.

"Mom?"

"Aruun?? Are you having an asthma attack?? Where are you? I expected you back by now. We're getting frantic here."

"I-I don't know where I am. I have to figure that out. Right now, I'm actually lost."

"What do you mean?! How did that happen?"

"I'll have to call you back when I'm—uh—oriented."

"Ok, call right back and we'll send a driver for you. Are you okay, honey?"

She hadn't called him that in years. He blinked quickly and swallowed a little too hard.

"Yeah. Just had a very unexpected adventure. I'll get back to you."

He shoved his phone back in his pocket and made sure his camera strap was still looped around his wrist. He gulped some air and stepped clear of the doorway into a dim pool of light.

"You are lost, perhaps?" said a voice. "I can help you. Where are you going?"

Aruun gazed straight into the face of this stranger, trying to assess his intention in this semi-darkness. He was tempted to accept his help. What was the alternative? The sputtering lights in the street enlarged his confusion and, for an instant, he could not summon the name of the hotel, or the Chandni Chowk market. He pulled his focus from the man's hairless face and looked away, as if this would cause the information to materialize. In the distance, his gaze fell upon a pot of fire down the road tended by an old woman wrapped in plain cloth and stillness. "Chandni Chowk," he then managed to say. He was drawn to the woman as she was drawn to her pot of flames He took a step in her direction. As his fingers instinctively curled around the camera strap the edge of a knife met his grip.

"AAAHH!" He crumpled, clutching his hand leaking blood. A boy swiftly dispatched the camera strap with the pocket knife. There was a crunch underfoot, probably Aruun's glasses. His senses exploded as he shoved his arms ahead on the stone pavement and lunged for the leg in front of him, catching it, digging his fingernails into the flesh of the boy's ankle until he screamed, flailing his leg to escape. But Aruun held on, yanking backwards. The boy stumbled, smashing his knee on the cobblestones as Aruun's cheekbone bounced on the pavement. They were both stunned, sprawling there together, Aruun's grip on the boy's ankle growing slippery with his own blood, his fingernails pushing deeper into the flesh of the ankle.

Then he heard the sound of footsteps—slow ones—and the voice of a woman shouting, louder and louder until it became the only sound there was. He rolled his eyes up and caught a glimpse of the raw edge of heavy plain fabric.

It was the woman from the fire pot. Her frail and gnarled form emitted a voice that could halt just about anything. He had been on the verge of approaching her, instead she had come to him. She continued yelling as she bent herself in half to snatch the camera, at which point Aruun released the ankle in his grip. As the boy struggled to his feet, the woman gave him a hard shove. He stumbled a few steps, grabbed his knife from the cobblestones, then limped away.

With difficulty, Aruun rose off the pavement as he felt a gentle hand on his back. The woman was barely five feet tall. At five-foot-six, Aruun towered over her. Mute and shaken, his hand oozed blood and his face throbbed where it had struck the stones. In silence, the woman led him to her booth where stacks of clay pots stood like sentinels and the fire still blazed in perfect containment. She motioned Aruun to a stool, then busied herself with supplies, muttering quietly.

He hunched forward and looked deep into the fire to steady himself. Within the shifting flames, he searched for something that might resemble the meaning of today's drama, or maybe even hints of his history. But all he saw was constant movement and the insistence of light. Without his glasses, the world had become an impressionist painting, halos of colors and wavy shapes, devoid of clear boundaries and definition.

The woman looked up and contemplated him with her milky brown eyes. He felt her gaze settling lightly upon him like a fine cloth and so he, too, looked up, wondering how much she could actually see through her cataracts. How could she have noticed the attack going on many stones away? Maybe she could see a great deal beyond the confines of her eyesight. If only he could as well.

She was speaking to him in Hindi (maybe), or so he guessed. How weird that he didn't recognize the major language of his birth country. In response to her, he extracted a wrinkled piece of paper from his wallet and read the words out loud: *Main hindi naheen boltaa hoon* ("I do not speak Hindi"). "English. I was born here," he said pointing to the ground with the index finger of his good hand. Then he placed his palm on his chest. "My name is Aruun." She nodded, without a note of surprise or understanding. She continued murmuring quietly as she poured hot tea into little ceramic cups without handles.

Aruun awkwardly picked his water bottle out of his belt pack and soaked the napkin from the market with the remaining water, using his left hand to clean the wounded right one. The woman watched him struggle and then she reached for his hand to continue dabbing away the blood. The wounds were clearly visible now—deep cuts nearly unmasking bone—and she raised his hand two inches from her eyes to examine it in detail. Aruun saw the raw, gaping openness and his stomach revolted. He far preferred the covering of blood to the sight of his own torn flesh.

The woman knelt on the ground and reached forward with difficulty, scuttling pots aside until she found the one she wanted tucked behind the rest. As she brought it closer, Aruun could smell the fermented liquid swimming with small green leaves as she swirled a cloth in the brew, wrung it out, and applied it to his cuts. He tried desperately to welcome this new scent, to believe that it was just the first aid he needed, but instead was consumed with dread that it would cause a massive and incurable infection. Or, at the very least, that the smell of this brew would linger with him forever and become his new signature fragrance.

She folded his fingers over the compress. Then squinting her eyes and pursing her lips, facial muscles converging into a mass of wrinkles, she turned her attention to his cheek, barely touching it. He meant to flinch, but did not.

She dipped her fingers into her medicinal mix and dabbed it on his bruised cheekbone. Her dry and deeply ridged hand lingered and Aruun closed his eyes. He had the sense that his skin was laying against the bark of an ancient tree. When he opened them again, their eyes were steady for one another. *"Potii"* she said, *"Potii."* He did not understand, and it hurt too much to smile.

Aruun nodded slightly. He could hardly hear her anyway and his eyes were tearing from the smoke as the fire between them diminished. The woman's eyes shimmered with moisture, and they sat like this for a small collection of moments in the warm and receding glow of flaming pots and medicinal aromas.

Suddenly, Aruun remembered that he had never called his mother back. He wrestled his phone out of his pocket and tried the number, but the charge was no longer strong enough and the call failed. His mind careened forward—by now he had certainly ruined everyone's trip. His parents would never forgive him for wasting their money. They would regret they had ever adopted him. His mother would leave India without him, and he would be swallowed up in Delhi forever, scrambling to survive and...

He was sweating profusely in the evening heat, waiting for a solution to present itself, to intrude like a welcome stranger, parting the curtains on his burgeoning headache and blunted thinking skills. His best thought was to stay where he was until dawn and somehow find transport back to the hotel.

By now the fire was out, and the light from the naked street bulbs was the single source of illumination. As footsteps slowly advanced toward them, shivers of hope and apprehension consumed him. A misshapen man materialized and exchanged a few words with the woman, who gestured once in Aruun's direction, maybe providing an explanation for the presence of this stranger who seemed to have dropped in from a distant planet for a brief visit. The man withdrew with a curt nod.

Time passed, and Aruun sat helplessly on his perch watching while the woman put her shop to sleep for the night. Off to the side, he could barely make out a statue with a head in the shape of an elephant on a tiny alter surrounded by fruits and small dishes of honey. Or maybe it was his imagination. The world was blurry. He watched as the woman scooped what looked like rice and flower petals out of a nearby pot and lifted her hands over the statue. As her gnarled fingers splayed open, grains of rice in a shower of petals drifted down over the altar while she chanted words he did not know from a world he longed to recall.

All of a sudden, it struck Aruun that he was only half help-less—he still had one good hand. He quickly stood up and began moving pots one at a time while the old woman indicated to him where they should be placed behind the back curtain. Relieved to be in motion, he was glad he could work to repay her enormous favor. The sound of one pot meeting the inside of another brought a sort of music in place of a conversation they could not have.

He became so absorbed in this new soundscape that he missed the faint but growing voices in the distance. Although the woman's vision was cloudy, her hearing was still keen. As she looked in the direction of the voices she stepped out of the booth, stretching and waving with great effort. It was then he finally heard "Aruun! Aruun!"

As the shouting steadily gained volume, he realized it was the voices of two women, one dusky, one shrill, colliding, overlapping. "Aruun!! ARUUN!!!"

His mother.

And Navya.

Wow.

The woman stepped into the street and faced the voices, continuing her slow wave. Aruun followed, straining to see the faces, but all he could recognize was his mother's unmistakable way of walking, now running, feet turned out, flapping against the stones. He walked toward her at a snail's pace, wrapped in unreality as she grabbed him, sobbing. He was trembling and swallowing over and over again, but she couldn't have noticed. Navya was crying into her hands.

Aruun stepped back. "Wait—I don't get it. How did you find me?"

"Locate Any Phone," said Navya in her crisp accent. "Something we've never had to use before. But, thanks to you, now we know it works."

"Ohhh…" he said quietly. "If I had known, I wouldn't have been such a train wreck."

"You and me both," said his mother, pushing her hair out of her eyes as she scrounged around her bright green bag for a tissue. "Please don't ever do that again. Promise?!" She looked at him harder this time. "Oh my God, what happened to you?!?"

She had just noticed his bandaged hand.

"And where are your glasses?"

"Smashed. Over there. There's a story. But first, I want you to meet my new…uh…friend. I owe her a lot of gratitude—and I don't even know her name."

They walked over to her as she smiled slightly and dipped her head. "Akanksha" was all she said. Was that her name?

Corinne took both her hands and leaned forward earnestly, "Thank you, thank you, thank you," before she even knew quite what she was thanking her for. Aruun carefully managed his camera with his right hand and took some pictures as Navya spoke to the woman. As they learned that Aruun had been attacked, his rescuer turned his palm over to display the slashed flesh.

"Well we better get this boy to Urgent Care," Corinne said. But as the three turned to leave the woman called after them, "Aruun!" She reached inside the waistband of the underskirt of her sari and drew out a small pouch which she offered to him. He hesitated, but she urged it upon him with a small push and a nod. He bowed slightly and slipped the pouch into his front pocket.

The cab took them to Urgent Care, where they waited for hours Aruun came out with seven stitches. By the time they returned to the hotel, everyone in their group had long since gone to bed. Aruun and some of the others would be leaving before dawn for the airport, but unfortunately Holly would not be among them. This was not how he had imagined his goodbye.

The plane ride home was a blur of mediocre snacks accompanied by a mix of Aruun's own playlist and airplane white noise—all punctuated by a string of restless naps and unwelcome wake-ups. No reading or movie could hold his focus. His mother was either respecting his need for quiet or was so exhausted herself that all she could manage was to stare blankly at the screen or doze in the cradle of her red neck pillow. Their major conversation had taken place in the waiting room of the urgent care clinic, so she was caught up on the details of last night's story, but their exchange had not included what had transpired for either of them within the chambers of heart and mind.

Life looped around and took shape again, obscuring the trip to India until it wasn't clear that it had really happened at all. Aruun's dad Brad saw the pictures and asked a few questions, clearly regretting that he had decided to miss the chance to share the experience due to the expense factor. Aruun returned to classes at the junior college, Brad and Corinne to their jobs and to their involvement with the Beacon of Hope Adoption Circle.

And therein lay the rub.

One day in late January, on a Sunday evening after enjoying a cordial enough dinner together, his parents approached him with a small request.

"Hey Aruun," his dad began. "You know we're pretty active in BHAC. I'm on the board and all. Great bunch of folks, and we have a lot in common."

"Yeah, so…"

His mom chimed in. "Next month we're hosting a gathering here for prospective adoptive parents, and everyone would love it if you'd be the featured speaker. February 18th. Put it on your calendar, okay?" She smiled, tilting her chin up playfully.

"What?!" Aruun frowned as he replied, pulling his own chin back and down. "C'mon…I really have zero to report, and I am definitely not a public speaker. As you know."

"It's not about public speaking. First of all, there will only be about a dozen or so people, all super nice. And it's not at all formal, just in our living room, you know, and you can totally be yourself. Maybe talk about the trip, too. You have all those great snapshots."

"Snapshots?" he said. "You mean do a travelogue?! Sounds like something you'd be good at. It would be so much fun for *you*!"

"C'mon, Aruun," his father cajoled, with a growing edge of impatience. "Stop dragging your feet. It would be awesome sharing your experiences with these folks. Going back to your homeland and all."

"Sharing my experiences?" he said. "What does that even mean? And why would I want to share anything with strangers anyway? I have nothing in common with them. Find someone else for this job. It won't be too hard with all your many contacts, I'm sure."

He turned and walked toward his room.

"Now you wait just a minute," his dad yelled after him. "Hey, buddy, we financed your trip to India, in case you forgot that little fact."

Aruun wheeled around. "Oh, so that's it. I get it. I owe you. Now at least you're being truthful. Okay, now it's *my* turn to be clear: I AM NOT YOUR POSTER BOY."

Corinne's eyebrows shot up to her hairline. She ran after him, barely catching his bedroom door before he slammed it. "Aruun, what's got into you lately? You used to be so agreeable. Now, all of a sudden, you're so argumentative. Don't be like that! Really, it would mean so much to us, and to the group."

"You know..." Aruun started to say, turning to look at her, contemplating her hazel eyes set in that translucent white skin, her finely chiseled, lightly freckled nose—feature for feature having nothing to do with him. "On second thought, I'm going out." He strode past them toward the door and exited.

"Where are you going??" never even reached his ears.

And actually, he didn't know where he was going. He texted his best friend Cheyenne, a mildly crazy representative of the theater crowd and a senior in high school. He liked the way her emotions were all out there, while his were squirreled away. She opened the doorway to the feeling world for him while he provided a sort of container for her ever-surging emotions. His phone beeped: "YEP, now's good!!"

The fifteen-minute walk seemed like an hour. He had left hastily without any thought of a coat, and it was 28 degrees outside. At last he arrived at the small gray house Cheyenne shared with her mom (an outbuilding, actually, of a much larger gray house) and she appeared wearing an array of sweaters, scarves, and mismatched socks—if you included the hair streaks, possibly 18 colors in all. She saw Aruun standing there with his hands stuffed in his pockets, coatless.

"OMG, come in right now," she shrieked. She threw her arms around him in hopes of warming him in all her fabrics and backed them both across the threshold into the toasty kitchen. He gently extricated himself.

"My mom is at Aunt Julie's. She'll be back sometime, I don't know. Let's sit in here, ok?" She motioned to the kitchen. Of course. It was where they always sat. "And you can tell me what the hell is going on that you would walk over here without a coat. Must be something pretty SPECTACULAR," she said waving her arms above her head. Her voice was just a tad too loud, but he was glad to be there.

As he told her the story over a cup of hot canned soup, she was uncharacteristically quiet.

Then she said in a low tone, "You should so do this."

"Exactly *what* are you talking about?? I mean, did you forget whose side you are supposed to be on??"

"No," she said simply. "Yours."

"Well, then I guess you better explain."

"It's not about your parents. Or impressing these people they probably want to impress."

"Yeah...and your point?"

"I just think you could make a really cool presentation. You'll have an audience to hear what you want to say, complete with the visuals—all those amazing pictures you took on your trip. Plus, I'll help you, and what could be better?!?"

"Hey, you're the one who's looking for the audience. You got us confused," he said opening, closing, and circling his clicking jaw.

Cheyenne leaned forward. "Hey, so what? Just because I crave attention and you don't doesn't mean you don't deserve it." She smiled, "Pretty good, huh? Now what are you gonna say to that?"

"The same thing: NO DOG AND PONY SHOW. Sorry to disappoint you and Corinne and Brad all in one blow."

"Oh, stop the drama and have some more soup," she said going to the pantry for a second can of tomato basil. "I know, I know—funny line coming from me."

She got a smile from him, but not a change of mind.

"Oh, say something Aruun," Cheyenne pleaded after a one-minute silence that strained her tolerance level. "What are you thinking? Nothing critical of the soup, I hope."

"I *was* actually thinking about the soup. That I like it better than my messed up family at the moment, even though it was born in a tin can."

"Wait a minute!" she said. "At least your mother is the same age as your dad. My stepmom is more like a generation different—how adorable that I could call her 'sis.' Now *that* is truly messed up."

"She's your stepmom, not your mom. And not extremely adorable, I realize. But no one is pressuring you to be grateful every time you turn around. That makes you truly blessed!"

The door opened, and Cheyenne's biological mom walked in. She threw her keys on the counter and tossed her coat over the red railing to the upstairs.

"Hey, Aruun. How *are* you?" She shared that same overblown voice with her daughter, but wore fewer colors. The overall effect was quieter, though still tipping toward chaos. She sipped a cup of coffee. "I forgot about this and left it in the car. Iced café at this point. Oh, well," she said wobbling her curly head to and fro. "Still works."

Aruun stood up. "Hey, I'm good. How're you doing?"

"Liar…" muttered Cheyenne. Her mom was bending over the kitchen table, shuffling through the mail that was still strewn and stained with food drippings from days ago, totally missing the comment. Aruun pulled out his phone by habit.

"Actually, I have to get back. Thanks for the soup."

"Waitwaitwait," said Cheyenne. "Now that you've thawed out, let's keep it that way, shall we? I'll drive you."

"Offer accepted," Aruun said. "So long, Monica."

"Bye," she answered, flashing a wide smile. "Soon, Aruun."

"Mom, stop that. It's rude."

"Aruun knows I'm just being friendly."

"Yeah, maybe."

"We're good. No worries," Aruun said while Cheyenne grabbed her coat, crammed in her many layers, and snatched the keys as they left.

It was a brief and quiet ride to his house. When they stopped in front, Cheyenne turned off the engine before she spoke. "Seriously, reconsider your refusal. Even if your parents think this is for them, turn it into something else. WITH. MY. HELP."

"Thanks for the ride." He got out without the merest glance in her direction.

The house was dead quiet. His mom was posing on the couch for his benefit, he figured, apparently absorbed in a book titled *20 Things Adopted Kids Wish Their Parents Knew*. His dad had vanished upstairs, no doubt glued to his computer screen.

Corinne looked up from the page, carefully holding the book cover in plain view and regarded Aruun over her red-framed readers. "Nice to see you."

"Yup."

"Listen," she ventured quickly before he disappeared. "The presentation isn't for a month. You have time to think it over and do just whatever you want with it. We won't censor you."

"Thanks for the pep talk, Mom, but I don't need time to think it over. I'm done."

She didn't answer. He went in his room, shut the door, and sat on his bed next to the black jacket that was still laying there wondering why it had been left behind on a cold night. He put it on for some reason and continued to sit, swamped with emptiness.

The closet was in his sight line, with the plaid rolling bag he had taken to India shoved in the back. His gaze took in the dings and scuff marks, souvenirs from his homeland, it was a miracle that it still zipped and rolled. It was a miracle that he still zipped and rolled too, considering all the stress. With a bit of a jolt, he realized the bag was still only partially unpacked.

Aruun rolled it out of the closet and began rummaging through the outer pockets. Empty. He flipped open the main compartment and dumped the contents on the floor. He shook out a few crumpled shirts that were ripe (okay, overripe) for the wash and a small packet of mustard seeds tumbled out. Oh yeah, this was a gift for his parents not yet given. There was also a small tan cloth pouch. Amidst the haze of jet lag, healing hand and cheekbone, not to mention the weirdness of re-entry into a life he that he used to know as "normal," this little sack had completely escaped his mind. Now, he grabbed it. The drawstrings were pulled tightly together like the strands of India memories that he had barely loosened since his return to Massachusetts. Now, with less than full finger strength, Aruun had to work to pry the physical strings open. How strange that he could have forgotten about this gift from Akanksha. His own brain was sometimes the most alien terrain.

The strings finally parted, and he drew out a small clay form with an elephant head. Memory lights started flickering. His rescuer. Her altar. Flower petals. Rice. Milk. Aruun set the tiny figure down on his desk and turned to the internet to search. "Ganesha: Remover of obstacles; seat of wisdom, knowledge and new beginnings." He stared at the screen trying to extract some personal meaning.

His phone buzzed with a message. "And how was homecoming?" Cheyenne, keeping tabs.

He decided to call back in hopes she could decode for him with her fantastic imagination. He related the story of his forgotten gift.

"Wow," she said softly. "Amazing. You now possess the power to 'remove obstacles and create new beginnings.'"

"Wait, wait," Aruun answered. "I think I know where this is going. Just watch your step there." Nevertheless, he felt his body lighten with their connection, even in disagreement.

"I'm not looking to remove obstacles. Things are chill the way they are."

"Oh, really?!" she said. "How's your home life? And why haven't you told me much about your trip?"

"Hey, I've been tired. Why do you actors make such a big fucking deal out of everything?"

"Yeah, I know, and it's been freezing outside, too. C'mon, Aruun, then how come you fled your house tonight without bothering to put on a jacket? 'Cuz everything's FANtastic. Nothing in your way. Just lookin' for good conversation?"

"You're being a brat, you know that?"

"I guess I do know that. It's my way of trying to get you off your butt and..."

"And what??"

"And DO something with all you've just gone through. All the memories, all the experiences and materials that are right in front of you waiting for you to rummage through, to look and feel and..."

"Whoa, ok, thanks. This is getting out of hand. Too much drama. Getting off now. Good night."

"Are you hanging up?"

"In a manner of speaking.

"Well...love you anyway."

"Got it. Thanks."

Click.

Days passed as they are inclined to do. Aruun went to classes, mostly wearing a jacket, sort of keeping up with his schoolwork, and kind of conversing with his parents when they crossed paths—but never about the looming Beacon of Hope event. Things were frosty at home, words were sparse, eye contact minimal. In fact, it was as if a real chill enveloped him regardless of where he was or the current temperature. Since the homeland trip, Aruun had resumed a life of going through the motions which didn't autocorrect with the easing of jet lag as he had hoped.

One afternoon, after slinging his leg over his bike, Aruun steered in the direction of home. He stopped at the corner of Alden Street but hesitated to cross on green as usual. Instead, he rested the toe of his boot on the pavement and took out his phone. *"Meet 4 caffeine?"* he texted Cheyenne. Her high school day was over. Hopefully, she wasn't rehearsing for yet another thing. He waited.

In a moment his phone lit up. *"Gimme ½ hr. See you @ Artsy."*

He wheeled his bike around and headed left on Alden Street. He'd wait for her at the coffee shop, hopefully at a window table so he could stare through it when their conversation stalled. He actually didn't know what he wanted to talk about, only hoped that soon it would occur to him. Maybe the moment Cheyenne appeared, all his brain lights would go on and his own breath would begin to warm him again.

He managed to nab a decent table next to a window with a view of a leashless black dog focusing patiently on the door of the cafe. It was amazing how composed the dog was, how unquestioning his trust in the return of the owner he could not see. Unimaginable, Aruun thought, that kind of unwavering faith in security.

A cold draft sped toward him from the entrance.

"Hey, did you see that dog just sitting there, not tied up or anything?" called a familiar, outsized voice from the door. "I could definitely not be trusted to sit still that long if I were that dog."

"Or believe that the owner would ever come back."

"Yea, that would be the second problem. Anyway, HI. So glad you rang!"

Aruun came close to smiling as Cheyenne dumped her backpack and two of her five scarves with excess fringe. They went to the counter to order, both happy to see there was no line.

Back at the table, Aruun watched the dog's face change, ears tilting forward when the owner opened the door of Artsy Cafe and walked out. The stillness dissolved into tail and then whole-body wagging. "I just knew you'd come!" it seemed Aruun could almost hear him say. *Man, I am so out of it,* he said to himself. *Now I think I hear animals talking.*

But by then Cheyenne had jumped in, "God, he might as well be talking: 'Great to see you again, bro'! I never took my eyeballs off that door, I promise!'"

"Just what I was thinking, believe it or not," Aruun said. "Except that I thought I had actually heard him talk, unlike you who said, 'might as well be.'"

Chuckle. Pause.

"So why did you text me?"

"I needed caffeine and who better to share it with?"

"C'mon," she said, rolling her eyes 180 degrees north. "What. Is. Up. Man?"

Aruun raked his fingers through his hair. "Uh, I don't know where to start."

"I don't care. Just start somewhere," she countered. "We've got till eight till they kick us out."

The conversation meandered slowly, but then finally caught momentum. Framed by the window were two heads inclining toward one another as time unrolled and Aruun scratched his pen on a notepad. They split a second cup of coffee. Cheyenne's fingers danced on the keys of her laptop. Steam obscured their window. They kept the table until closing when they were politely kicked out.

• • •

February 18th, Corinne and Brad's living room.

Amidst the chatter about the plusses and minuses of adoptee-sending countries like Ethiopia, Haiti, and Peru, Aruun and Cheyenne arose together out of the corner of the living room, a flash mob of two. Cheyenne busied herself with the Power Point and Aruun positioned himself in front of the newly blank wall he had arranged as people gradually quieted down and turned their attention toward him. Corinne regarded Aruun quizzically, a mixture of pride and alarm on her face, her eyebrows not quite knowing where to settle. Brad sat in the big green upholstered chair with his arms folded across his chest, his face as blank as the wall in front of him.

With the click of a mouse, Cheyenne filled the wall behind Aruun with a distant shot of the garbage dump. No explanation was offered.

"Hey, guys. I'm Aruun" he began, pacing back and forth in his two and a half feet of available space. You don't know me. But I'm here to tell you we've got some things in common.

"You and I, we both came into shiny worlds, our little bodies glistening with anticipation.

"Your world shone from polished floors, steel equipment, fluorescent lights, and the gleam in your mothers' eyes.

"Blinding lights for me came from the blazing sun catching on foam slippers, aluminum cans, and shards of glass—mother's eyes nowhere.

"We each have our beginnings.

"You and I, we were wrapped up from the start for our protection. Maybe you remember: You were in a clean flannel blanket warmed specially by the hospital machine that heats to the perfect temperature.

"I was in a filthy gray rag chosen especially for me, to be heated without mercy by the sun and whipped open by the wind, in the garbage dump of my beginnings."

He nodded toward the wall now displaying a closer view of the same scene.

"You were welcomed with love—into the arms that would carry you home and onward into childhood.

"And this is where we part company. It is the fork in our road.

"Oh, make no mistake, I too was cradled. But in arms forever unknown—and placed so very carefully among the discarded shiny objects. Placed with care, with desperate hope.

"And, dare I imagine, with love.

"This is the rubble of my beginnings. It is where we part ways, you and I. I have clawed the tiny shards of my story out of the nothingness and come up with but a fraction of my history.

"Yours, presented to you on a platter, is whole and completely your own.

"The rubble of my beginnings, the heap of the broken and discarded, is mine. I have seen it now and I will never let it go.

"You can pretend, but cannot make me pretend, that coming here to this land means everything. I mean, here never cancels there, the before never disappears from view.

"Oh, we can make nice and talk gratitude, but my story is not to be erased or ignored. Look," he said, pointing to the image on the wall. "It's too late. I have already claimed it."

"Hey, I'm not saying your lives have been shiny perfect.

"And I'm not even saying I'm not grateful for what has come after my rough start.

"Well then, you wonder, so where is the gratitude in this lucky boy?

"My first mother gave me life, and these parents here who sought me and caught me have made sure that my life unfurled from this other land. They have set an open path of opportunity before me that I recognize as good fortune that might never have been.

"It's true.

"But now I have laid my eyes on the discard and felt the shock of it run through me like a megawatt bolt.

"I have surveyed the pieces before me until they broke me down to lay among them, raw and alone. All now crystallized into an indescribable taste alive on my tongue every day.

"But don't get me wrong. Flashing these dump images at you is not a plea for your pity. It's not for shock value. My confession is this: I am actually trying to penetrate your fantasy-fogged brains about adoption.

"Learning is possible, and it's a big have-to. But not just for kids. For you guys who want to adopt kids too. Let me say our past cannot and should not be erased. Get on board with that in a deep way, or please don't do this. Go to Plan B.

"You might wonder how any of us can carry the stone in our hearts that is an untold story, a history which is our entitlement but has vaporized instead, been discarded without our permission. The answer is this: With or without words, we adoptees bear it together.

"My bones tell me that like most birth moms, mine never wanted to give me up and disappear.

"We share one heart broken in two.

"That broken heart is my doorway where the light is beginning to come through. The light of honest feeling, so raw sometimes that it scares both of us, you and me. The light of the anger that is mine. Of the sadness I carry for my mother—and all mothers forced to lose their kids—of sadness for never knowing her and the love that I believe was there. Is there.

"My anger bleeds into sadness, my sadness into longing, my

longing into thankfulness, because my mother chose life, my life with all those feelings that I carry, that sit at my table and feed me, that make me real every single day.

"My sadness and my gratitude are brothers. They hang together.

"For all this, I am truly grateful.

"And this is my offering to you all."

Upon the wall a close-up appeared of a woman gazing into a pot of fire, her lined face and clouded eyes barely visible through the leaping flames. Then, in a flash, the image went dark, and the presentation was over.

Except for the sound of Cheyenne shutting down and packing up the computer, the room was quiet. No comments or questions or gathering of things. Aruun hovered, awaiting a response, but was okay without one—he had said what he needed to say, and left it there for the taking.

END NOTES

1   "Why Gratitude Is Good," greatergood.berkeley.edu, November 16, 2010.

2   "Please don't tell me I was lucky to be adopted,"by Shaaren Pine, *Washington Post Magazine*, January 9, 2015.

3   "The Bad Adoptee," nofoghere blogspot (This blog has apparently been taken down since I first came across it.)

4   "Who is Entitled to my Gratitude?" Declassified Adoptee blog, Amanda Transue-Woolston, February 13, 2013.

PICK UP YOUR PEN

What comes to mind when you hear the word "gratitude"?

_____
_____
_____
_____
_____
_____
_____
_____

Are there complications?

_____
_____
_____
_____
_____
_____
_____

How free are you to say what is true for you?

_____
_____
_____
_____
_____
_____
_____
_____

Given how beneficial gratitude is, how integral to happiness, how can we foster it without sacrificing other emotions that are equally real?

_____

_____

_____

_____

_____

_____

_____

_____

_____

_____

Illustration by Addie Bara

Belonging

"The big topic of my life has been fitting in. THE big subject of my life. I'm always trying to find people I can relate to."—Niko

S EEKING COMMON GROUND. Fitting in. Connecting. Ideas that blossom on the surface while the roots probe deep underground.

As human beings we are wired to be interdependent for our very survival. We have an instinct and universal need for connection—whether or not it's available in the ideal form.

Belonging, connection, kinship and rootedness. For transnational adoptees, these words can be loaded and the terrain they describe can be rocky. As one adoptee expressed it, "Can you imagine being the only person in the world you know you're related to?"

"Living in a house full of strangers" is how author/therapist/adoptive parent Nancy Verrier describes the sense adoptees often have of their adoptive families.[5] Or as one intercountry adoptee put it:

∾

"Not a lot of people understand what it's like growing up in an environment that is totally alien to you...Then when you get old enough to ask questions, you end up questioning everything about yourself because you don't know who you are."— Anonymous

∾

Even within a family where there is caring, commitment and closeness an adoptee may still feel on the outside of the circle looking in, rather than in the innermost space of the family. This is not necessarily about lack of love. Although adoptive parents might not experience this distance themselves, the question still hangs in the air for many international adoptees: Where is the assumption of belonging? When adoptions begin with separation from first families and/or first cultures it's understandable that assumptions about belonging might have been wobbly from the start.

The feeling of being different from those closest to you can create an undercurrent of chronic unease. After all, not only do all adoptees have roots outside their adoptive families, but most international adoptees are children of color joining white families, often in predominantly white communities—a natural set-up for alienation. When there are no human reference points, like an older or younger version of yourself, no one around who mirrors you in physical features or personality traits, it can be confusing and lonely.

Many questions ride on this complex and weighty word "belonging." What does it even mean? How do you go about finding it? Niko again:

"I find a lot of things to be funny that other people don't think are funny...I think because there are clear differences between myself and my family, that got naturally instilled. I mean, it's absurd to be in a family that looks nothing like you. You have to laugh sometimes. At least I did. You have to be funny in order to survive the adversity...I didn't talk with my family too much about it. I had to make sure when I was with my family that I wasn't different from my family. I didn't like talking about it because I felt like it separated me from them."

∽

"For as long as I can remember I felt lost in the U.S. Everyone around me seemed to be tall with blonde hair and blue eyes. I felt I didn't fit in anywhere. I tried fitting in. Many times it was a struggle for

me. *Am I Korean or American or both? It was hard for me growing up in America. I kept thinking there was something wrong with me inside. Most of my friends were of American background. In school, I only had one Korean adopted friend. I was always interested in Korean culture and the language.*

"I was very fortunate to be adopted into a very loving family. Yet I always felt a very large part of me was missing. I did not know why. I just felt it. I felt different, looked different and liked different foods, such as cucumbers and rice for breakfast!

"I have a very large Korean family in South Korea and it turns out that all of them thought that I died in the baby home. This greatly increased the feeling I had my whole life since my childhood—that I did not exist!" —KATIE AGRANAT[6]

~

"I first went back to Korea when I was 12. I remember sitting on the subway with my mom (who is about 5'9" with very fair skin and reddish brown hair) and looking around. Then it hit me that everyone else in the subway looked like me (except her) and that I could be related to any one of them (except her)."
—CHRISTINA SEONG[7]

~

More than one adoptee related the experience of friends commenting about how different they looked from their adoptive families. Such comments just underscored the fault line in their sense of belonging.

~

"My (adoptive) mom and I are so much alike...I hate telling people I'm adopted. I hate the word. I don't use it. I hate having anything that separates me from my family. I always felt that the word 'adopted' was a really negative thing. I won't ever identify with the

word. (Culture) camp is just about the only time of year when I use the word frequently." —MALLORY

~

"My sense of belonging is strongest with immediate family. I definitely get a good amount seeing aunts and uncles and stuff like that. It's funny, I did recently have a decent conversation about this with my (adopted) sister. She's pregnant, actually due any minute. It's really a big deal. I mean I am so happy for her. She's going to have her own flesh and blood. It's a lot more meaningful for us.

"We kind of talked about, too, growing up with aunts and uncles…I loved them all dearly. I loved being around them, but it definitely is sort of a disconnect in a way that I feel. It's not really in a bad way. I just never felt one of them. I don't know. It's hard to say without sounding completely negative. If I didn't see them for a long time, but—no offense—it wouldn't like break my heart. I don't know, but there is that weird disconnect that I don't share with my friends. My girlfriend is really close to her family and she gets really upset with me sometimes when I'm like really flippant about that. I can't relate at all. I do love my parents but it's never like a huge priority in a way.

"I don't know. This sounds super negative. Even me being defensive like that is my upbringing showing itself, this constant guilt. It's gotten a lot better. I used to feel guilty about that stuff." —DEVON

~

"You're either bonding or not bonding with your (adoptive) parents. It's a crap shoot. You can't expect that you bring home a foreign child and you're gonna be like them and they're gonna be like you or have anything in common. And that's like me and my adoptive mother. We're like oil and water. We just don't mix. We have nothing *in common. Learning how to navigate a relationship with an adoptive mother is challenging. It's not so natural. Do you have a good experience with your adoptive mother or don't you? Because that can be like another let down or another trauma.*

"I lived in an all-white neighborhood and I was like the black sheep. And even the adults in the neighborhood would make me feel unwelcomed. They would ostracize me and so would their kids. So it was a secret I would try to keep, but you couldn't keep that secret. I didn't look anything like my parents. There was so much shame...It was rough to be different... It was bad. I was bullied. I got into fights.

"Now as an adult I look back and see that the people who made fun of me, they are the ones who didn't come from such great homes. But as a kid it sucks to be different. So I get it now, but as a kid, it's like the end of the world. You just want to die." —MARLA

~

"I finally let go of the notion that my parents' people, the German, Scandinavian, Norwegians, that make my dad and sister's eyes such a brilliant blue, are only borrowed. They can be denied to me by sight alone.

"When I was younger, I accepted my adoptive family's heritage as my own because it was all I had. Thinking of me as coming from the same place as my parents and siblings was a way for me to feel connected to my family and community. I participated in and assimilated into my adoptive cultural traditions because I didn't really know what else to do. My alternative was to have nothing.

"...When you commit to trying to feel like you're the same as everyone around you, you have to sacrifice your difference. You don't get to think about it, you don't get to go looking for it unless you want to be accused of being ungrateful. You can shelve it and bury it and try to forget that it even exists. You can feel very successful at *your own denial, easily avoiding the true meaning of your sadness and anger...and rootlessness and separation.*

"Admitting that I had some other people to connect to meant that I would have to admit I was very, very different than my family."
—KEUM MEE[8]

∾

You had certain choices as a child who completely depended on your adoptive family. These are not the same as the options you have as a young adult, when you might find more room to find and be your authentic self. This might seem obvious, but it's easy to forget and make a habit out of assuming your choices are still as limited as they once were. Think again.

For those who must put some authenticity aside while growing up (and all the questions that come along with that) a sense of alienation from family, friends or homeland can develop. Trying to fit in as a survival strategy—molding yourself to your environment—is not destined to yield a deep sense of belonging. But it can create a feeling of safety for the time being. Which makes perfect sense. Maybe it's what you had to do back then.

The inherent differences between you and your family can twist themselves into negative feelings, like shame, perfectionism or fear. Having that disconnect between your outer and inner life, not feeling quite real or worthy, perhaps trying to live up to a story that is not your own. These can all erode a sense of belonging.

But you can move along and find others who understand these feelings and experiences from the inside out. It is possible to embrace a sense of difference as being interesting and a source of personal pride, part of the story that is uniquely yours to tell, re-tell and shape over time. Regardless of whether you were encouraged to do so from the beginning.

~

*"It was very touching to me to travel to Sri Lanka with a group of adoptees, but I was not given a choice. I saw my birth records in the hospital. Some adoptive families I knew burned the birth records and baby pictures. I was the only one in the group who could verify my birth... On this trip they found my birth mom. I did not want my adoptive mom to come with me to see her for the first time but she insisted. I was 16 at the time. My two moms cried in each others' arms and it was beautiful for me to see that. (I would say) never give up trying to find out where you came from." —*SAMANTHA*

~

"I don't recall a time when my parents sat me down and told me my story.

*I don't think there ever was...it was the kind of thing that was always just kind of there. When I was younger, they did like a Korean Christmas. But there was never really a time when they told me about it...I'm kind of thankful they didn't...I don't know, maybe things would have been different if they had...I would tell a younger kid to talk to their parents. If the parents are keeping information from the child, there could be deeper issues that need to be discussed." —*NIKO*

CHILL IN THE AIR

*"I think growing up, there were little traces of things here and there, clues that my parents did not want to discuss or disclose my background. Little things...like hiding my passport."—*KAI*

A certain silence or secrecy in the family around adoption topics may spring from a fear on the part of your adoptive parents that knowledge of your roots could disrupt your connection with them. There are times when what is *not* being said is the loudest sound in the room. And the silence around a child's origins can make the topic seem taboo. Rather than solidifying a sense of belonging in the family, it might have the (probably unintended) opposite effect.

~

"I remember one summer in college when I came home. My mother was quite ill at the time and nothing was planned for my birthday. I was quite sad and I remember thinking, 'I bet I'm not the only person who is sad on this day. There is another woman somewhere who has a very different take on this day.'...My adoptive parents never, ever said the words 'birth parent'. It was not part of the equation."— DIERDRE

~

"My older brother was adopted at age 5. He was dismissed from the home because he was too abusive. One day he just disappeared. There was no discussion. So the message I internalized was that I could be next

We adoptees leave so much unexpressed as teenagers: We're either trying to be perfect and excel to validate our adoption—or we push the limits of our parents' commitment by being outrageous. Either way, the authentic expression is suppressed."—KENNY

THE CHOSEN BABY AND OTHER TALES

Maybe you were offered a "chosen baby" tale about your adoption when you were a child: A mystical, magical story of how you were destined to join your adoptive family. Perhaps you were told that your birth parents loved you so much that they surrendered you to opportunities for a better life. Or perhaps the only story you had was born from your own imagination.

Before there was ever an adoption tale, there was another story—the true, actual story—that stands on its own. One that you may or may not be drawn to or that might not even be available for the telling. Still, it exists. It belongs to you and you to it, even if it seems unreal, unpretty or imperfect. And how you think and feel your way through exploring this over a lifetime, stepping out from the "chosen baby" tale that might have been offered to you in childhood, is your story as well.

This is another facet of belonging that begs for attention: Gathering the elements of your own story—whatever is available to you—and embracing it as uniquely yours. While none of us can re-author our histories, they do belong to us. We own them.

If you were internationally adopted, the reality is that you have two cultures (at least), two countries and two families. You might resonate with the words of adoptee Deann Borshay in the film "First Person Plural:"

"I had to choose one family over the other...there wasn't room in my mind for two mothers."

～

*"It's so important to take yourself on that journey. Whether it's speaking up to your parents, seeking therapy, journaling, visiting your homeland or meeting other adoptees." —*KENNY

～

Feeling states are not necessarily fixtures in our lives; emotions are fluid and fluctuate in their intensity. In the meantime, read, write, talk—with family members, if possible, and trusted friends. If feelings are overwhelming—if you are experiencing depression, anxiety or suicidal thoughts—seek out a therapist specializing in adoption.[9] But don't wait until you're at your lowest point to seek support or professional help. Painful emotions so often become more manageable in the presence of real understanding and a longer perspective than you might have at the moment.

There is no pre-packaged sequence to follow in your explorations. Wherever you start is the beginning. It takes time, and it takes courage, to ask questions, to acknowledge vulnerabilities, to collect the fragments of your history. You have done what you needed to do to love and "adopt" your adoptive family, to adapt to your school and community. You have honed your exceptional survival skills and your resilience. These strengths will always be there to serve you whenever you begin this part of your journey and onwards.

Sometimes the desire to explore your history and heritage begins with a change of circumstance or event, like going to college, a family illness, a break-up, a homeland visit, a wedding, or the birth of a baby. Sometimes explorations take place in fits and starts. But they should always be taken in the spirit of befriending yourself. One person's rough start in life and another's smoother one does not define who deserves to belong and to be loved. Certainly our histories color our journeys—and no one else can describe those histories for us. As we absorb and speak our own stories, we begin to truly belong to ourselves.

When the mind wants to discover what the blood remembers, there can be obstacles. Like lack of information, resistance on the part of adoptive and/or birth families, your own fear or ambivalence, unsupportive friends—or even other adoptees who may feel threatened by the whole process of retrieving your personal history because they themselves are not ready to do the same. But if this is a journey that beckons you, find those who will be supportive. Go forward—and if there are naysayers, leave them behind.

$\sim$

"My college roommate was Puerto Rican and she came from a very strong East Coast cohort. And that was the first time that I noticed something was missing. She had something that I didn't...that sense of rootedness, of a historical continuum, of cultural belonging. I didn't feel rooted in anything. I thought I was missing out. That's when the grief and loss started for me. It really shaped her talks about her future, her relationships, her responsibilities That's when I realized I needed to figure it out, what does it mean to be Asian American, Korean American? How do you get that? Can you artificially create that for yourself?

"The grief and the loss really kicked in for me when I started having my own kids. I thought, 'I'm having children in a vacuum.' I started to pursue finding multicultural settings. That's when I felt a really profound loss, trying to create this for my kids.

"It created some distance with my adoptive family. We look different from you, we have a different history from you. They had no understanding of why I was making choices I did, to live in a multicultural neighborhood, to work in the adoption world. They were not supportive when I went to Korea for the first time. Their lack of support just created more distance. It could have been a bonding experience, but they did not want to hear about it. Kids I work with are having these feelings much earlier (middle school): 'You don't get me', 'you don't understand my life.'" —DIERDRE

⁓

"We (adoptees) have the disadvantage of having questions that we will never figure out. A lot of it for me is being honest. We may never know and it sucks, but that may be how it is for the rest of your life.

"A lot of kids fantasize about their birth families, some very extensive. I think most kids do...

"I'm also a huge advocate of therapy (with a therapist who

specializes in adoption). I'm so glad my mom put me in therapy. A lot of adoptive families are so freaked out about therapy. I don't know why."—MALLORY

VENTURING HOME

Here is Mallory again, this time on her momentous birth country visit:

"When I was 15, I was ready to go...It was a pretty incredible trip. My orphanage was actually closed down a year after I was adopted so we went to another orphanage which was wonderful. I had a blast at that orphanage. I didn't want to leave at the end of the day. We went to another orphanage in Calcutta which I did not like. It was dirty and I was kind of disgusted by it. But I loved the kids. But that orphanage didn't make an imprint on me like it did for the kids in my group who were from Calcutta. I'm from Madras.

"(That trip) was definitely a real eye-opener. It was emotional not only for me, but for my family as well. Seeing my mom experience that, seeing all those children, seeing her expressing that emotion made me realize how much our parents don't express things for our benefit. That, to me, is the most selfless thing.

"The letter that my birth mom wrote when she signed me over to the government I didn't actually see until I was an adult. I knew all the information contained in the letter. I knew her name and where in south India she lived. She tried to keep me for three weeks, but she wasn't married and the social stigma was really intense so that was the main reason—that was THE reason—she gave me up.

"There was one period when I was 11 and I was really curious (about searching). My mom's direct answer was 'Ok, we can. She had signed for you not to, but we can do it.' But then I said, 'Never mind.' I don't know why. Since then I have no desire to. I feel like I'd be running into a stranger who knew nothing about me, but looks

kind of like me. I feel no connection to her except she gave birth to me. I feel like I'm talking about a stranger when I'm talking about her. I have no clue about her."

⁓

"Even though I was just dumped by my birth mother in a box on the street, I will always feel connected with her and with my birth culture. How could it be otherwise?" —KELSEY

⁓

Your curiosity, your intuition or longing might draw you forward into your own specific story. When it does, you might discover how your experience mirrors those of other adoptees, regardless of whether or not you were born in the same country. Whatever elements of your story are known to you can be deeply meaningful, even as they are colored by frustration and loss. In exploring those connections that occur between people whose stories are not identical, but still connected, a new sense of belonging is within reach. All adoptees are linked by a common thread of implicit understanding or, in the words of Korean adoptee and Professor Kim Park Nelson, "share the same ghosts."[10]

⁓

"As Korean adoptees we have the same issues, perhaps shown in a more subtle manner. Native Koreans often feel 'sorry' for us, pity us, but still don't want us marrying their son/daughter. I have ambivalent feelings towards them. Wanna be with them, feel left out and resentful of them. Blame them for having the attitude, yet want to be like them. That's why fellow adoptees have my love, my respect, and my word that I will always defend and fight for them. They are more real to me than Koreans (who live in Korea) and every other group. They are my nation, and through them I have a country of my own." —EUN MI [11]

∽

There is no replacement for connection with other adoptees. While the understanding and interest of other friends and family members are very important, the knowing that comes from the related experience of another seems most often to be the most deeply validating. In the words of D.C. Wolfe in the film *Operation Babylift*, "It was a rebirth meeting other adoptees."

∽

*"I enrolled in a graduate creative writing program where I seriously began to seek answers to the losses I felt so deeply: 'Why was I adopted...Who were my biological parents? I sent out birth parent search forms to no avail. I trolled adoptee websites and began to get a clearer picture of the collective grief many adoptees feel. Guilt too." —*AMY LEE SCOTT[12]

∽

*"I met this guy in Chicago. One of his children is adopted...He had looked up my music and was touched by it. He sent me an email about the camp and his email was very filled with emotion and I was very moved. And I knew this was something I really needed to look into. I went to the camp and just had the best time. I had never been around so many adoptees and it was just the best experience for me... Everything stems from my adoption. It's my whole identity." —*NIKO

∽

"I have cribmates who were adopted and we all ended up in Colorado together. The four of us are pretty inseparable. One died this year, so it's been pretty hard. Even though none of us is biologically related, we shared a crib for two years and ended up living an hour from each other. I have three 'brothers'. We call each other 'brother' and

'sister'. I have a lot of adoptee kids who I talk to. Sometimes I'm jealous that I didn't have someone like that. They just tell me how they feel and I tell them it's ok. They know I get it and that's so important. Their parents would say it's ok, but it's different hearing it from someone who's been there." —MALLORY

~

Other adoptees talk about what a revelation it has been as adults to connect with other international adoptees: Having so much in common. Feeling free to ask questions: When were you adopted? Did you search for your birthmother? Or choosing not to tell your story. Feeling safe. Fitting in.

As one adoptee put it: "Issues of belonging, of yearning, of dealing with information denied or missing are all things that bind us together."

FINDING YOUR PLACE(S)

Knowing that you have access to both live kindred and virtual company gives you a community who will understand your experiences, feelings and questions about belonging.

Your exploration will probably not lead to absolute answers. There is no perfect single state of belonging. But there can be multiple belongings. And there is the distinct possibility of making peace with the two or more families and two or more cultures, that co-exist within you. In the words of one transnational adoptee interviewed, "If we never feel completely comfortable in one place, we feel comfortable in many places."

Your experience as an intercountry adoptee can expand your outlook and allow you to nurture inner resources of adaptability and resilience.

As one Colombian adoptee said, *"I think I have a greater perspective on the global community since I am a citizen of two countries and I have a complex nationality that encompasses two nations."*

~

"We have that ability to connect with a very diverse range of people. That's one thing that we (international adoptees) have an advantage of. I was always in the Exchange Student Clubs and I have a ton of friends all over the world. I'm definitely bonded with a lot of people with different backgrounds."—MALLORY

~

"Adoption has the dimension of connection—not only to your own tribe, but beyond widening the scope of what constitutes love, ties and family. It is a larger embrace... stretching past our immediate circles, and by reaching out, find an unexpected sense of belonging with others." —ISABELLA ROSELLINI[13]

~

At the center point of all of the circles of belonging in your life, you stand. Fully inhabiting your own unique and unfolding life story.

WHOLE LIFE HALF HIDDEN

Don't get me wrong. It's not like the snow was blood-stained or anything, although it might as well have been. It was just a few small black words on a stray piece of paper that had escaped the bundle of recycling I was hauling outside in the Colorado winter. Those words that scorched my brain then and even now. But as I said, there was no blood. Just a mere fragment of paper. Apparently, being the family recycler gives you access to closely guarded information that you wouldn't normally have. And as I was congratulating myself for spotting a piece of white paper in snow—which I would have normally ignored on purpose until spring thaw. I decided to pick it up, read it—and felt myself tipping over the brim of my own emptiness.

Clearly it was something official. Something medical. Something not intended for my eyes—yet as vital to me as my own bright red blood.

No one was home. Chips of white paint sprayed as I smashed the back door shut and went careening back into the house fleeing upstairs to my room. No hanging around the kitchen as usual mixing up some agreeable chitchat. Today I literally charged into my room, quickly, before my pulsing insides could burst through my pores. I closed the door firmly and took as deep a breath as I could manage.

I looked around as if the room were new. On the east wall of my room, I saw a rectangle shaped mirror leaning out, festooned with sweaters, sweatshirts and hats, some gray, some black. In the narrow vein of mirror that was still visible, I caught a glimpse of my reflection. Weirdly, my hair was still ultra-smooth, one strand laying down obediently next to the other, even after my whirlwind entrance.

By now my head felt like it might wobble loose and float away like that green balloon I lost to the wind when I was three—a complete heartbreak. I reached for the edge of my bed and lowered myself down with care. My eyes traveled around the walls of my bedroom smothered with photographs. Here were all the people I loved, yet their images were not calling to me in that moment. There were my blond-ish smiling parents, my cousins Nate and Lila, and my best friends Yolanda and Audrey. Grandpa and grandma (set #1) on their back porch, holding their glasses of iced tea and grandpa and grandma (set #2) in their golf outfits. Class pictures from first grade through tenth grade. Regional volleyball champions at McMillan Middle School. Lots of shots of me with my ready smile. People always like my smile. They say it is complete and total sunshine.

There were strips of color peering out uncertainly from between these photos. These were paintings of mine, rich colors doing their best to wake up the lavender walls of my perfect-teen-girl bedroom. My parents always encouraged me to include elements of Korea in my life, so I went along with that idea imbedding as much green as I could muster, because green is lucky in Korean culture. And I have a plant in my room with big leaves, which of course counts as even more green. For four summers in a row we all attended culture camp, which I actually did like. And I got to name our dog a Korean name, Miya. These things were all fine—but not overly.

My eyes darted from photo to photo until I came upon that picture of my dad and me on a spring day. Branches smothered in cherry blossoms arching over our heads, breezes mingling our light brown and jet black hair. Although he had me in a firm hold, my tiny hands clutched his ears with the conviction of one who always believes that an extra measure of security is paramount. I must have been ten months old in that picture, a mere two months after he had retrieved me from the airport and transported me to this spot I call home, where I learned to call them mom and dad. And to love them.

I stood a moment and let this image burrow in until it broke me open and tears began to pour. My dad, the one who anchored me to my existence, his very life was now in question. And I found out by accident.

A page discarded, not intended for my almond eyes, dropped, picked up again and read, informed me that he had a serious disease, so serious that he was in dire need of a kidney. And, sorry, there was no available donor at this time. The letter assured him that he was on a waiting list. In the meantime, suitable relatives should be sought. Right now.

"Suitable relative??" So what am I then?

I wiped my face with the back of my hand and settled on the cushion in the closet where I had a flashlight and a stack of shoe boxes. I was searching for something that would tether me to the ground which I had never felt was quite solid enough for me to stand on; more like sand with its shifting shapes and odd angles. People say I have a weird way of walking and standing, a little off-kilter because the soles of my feet don't completely touch. I even had physical therapy for this when I was younger, but all those exercises didn't make my feet believe the ground. The pediatrician and physical therapist just didn't get it—it was not about either my posture or my bones.

I pulled out the bottom box—the first of my secret stash launched by my eight year old self—and carefully lifted the lid.

The envelopes were all different sizes, strewn in a pile, half-sealed with plenty of crinkles. I had been here before. There was a box with "#1" written on it and I unfolded the page that was cradled there.

"This is the beginning of the story of my akshuel life. Well, akshuely, it began in Korea eight years ago. I was born somewhere I don't know where and left in a box in a dark alley near an orphanage. But I was lucky becuz someone found me and carried me into the orphanage where I stayed until the day I flew to the United States. I am named Felice which means happy, but not in Korean. French or something. Here is the green thread that was tied around my ankel in the box I was left and found in—by someone. Maybe my berth mother? Can you get fingerprints off a thread?"

I touched it lightly so as not to wear it too thin. How many touches could it bear without disintegrating? Amazing how a tattered little fragment, which remained with me only by the grace of one of the orphanage nannies, could be my greatest treasure. I closed my eyes as I always do and let it rest in the palm of my hand so I could feel its tiny pulse.

This was my private ritual, but today it did not calm me. Today I could not detect even the faintest pulse. I tucked the thread away.

Somehow it had never crossed my mind before that I could lose someone so close to me more than one time.

Box #2:

"Swimming today. Audrey and I moved up to Dolfins!! We're so excited. Afterwards a boy came up to me and asked where my mom was and she was standing right next to me."

Box #4:

"We're doing a play about holidays around the world. I got the part for Chinese New Year. But I don't want to wear a dragon costume. I want to be Uncle Sam for July 4th.

"Mom says I'm perfect for the New Year part and the kids will think it's cool. But I think they'll just remember that I'm different. Mom won't talk with Mrs. Beck about changing my part. She doesn't want to be the pushy parent. Pick your battles, she always says. But why not pick mine? I'm not even Chinese."

Box #5

"The play was awesome. That's what everybody said. I smiled and bowed. Mom and Dad took lots of pictures and bought the video. Melinda asked me how I learned to speak such good English. Mom said she was just being curious. I don't know if that's true or if there was something extra going on. Mom said, Let it go. How do you do that? She didn't tell me that part and I didn't ask. I guess I'll figure it out when I'm older, like 45 or so.

"We went for ice cream afterwards with Audrey's parents. I got Raspberry Mint. No one likes that except me. I wish I liked Cookie Dough, but I akshuely don't. We laughed, but I don't know about what. Audrey's mom Jenny said I have a pretty smile and that I should smile a lot. I know how to do that."

Box #6

"Here's my birthday note from Dad. It was under my pillow.

"You are the daughter I've dreamed of and your coming to us is magical. Happy 9th Birthday!
With love from your lucky Dad"

Pearls of sweat popped out on my forehead. Was there really something magical about this? Or was that just the giftwrap surrounding an empty box offered to me over and over again?

You can't automatically graft a stranger on to a family just like that. It's always a graft no matter what you say or do. Why had I been pretending to belong when now my situation was so completely clear? I told myself I was lucky to finally understand the reality of my situation.

The sound of dog paws scrambling across the kitchen linoleum. And then: "Felice?" my mom shouting cheerily. "Are you home, honey?"

I don't know. You tell me: *am* I??

I quickly ran a few strokes of the comb through my hair and splashed cool water on my face. Time to present myself as Felice. Leading a double life is part of my skill set. And it's not that I don't love my parents.

I led myself into the kitchen.

"Hey, Mom," I said managing a smile with the merest dose of eye contact.

"Oh, there you are. It was so quiet when I came home. No music blaring. Were you doing homework? How was your day? Did you have your physics exam?" She chattered in her friendly way, as if I were her next-door neighbor. "Could you please feed the pup? She's so hungry."

I sat on the floor with Miya who calmly molded her body into my lap. When you say her name "Me-a" it means "lost child" which is what I alone call her. I massaged her little starched ears and stroked her wiry fur until I could feel her starting to warm. And then the breath began to return to my body, too. This ragamuffin was found by the side of the highway and brought to the pound when she was just a handful of weeks old. Sometimes—actually lots of times—I feel like her littermate.

"She's not hungry for food," I said, "just a stroking."

"Well, ok, but please feed her soon?" requested Mom for the second time, every bit as friendly as the first. "And I'll feed *you*. How's that?"

"I'm not exactly hungry either."

"What's going on, honey? Are you ok?"

"How's Dad?"

"Oh, he'll be home in about an hour. Pretty tired from a demanding day, I imagine."

"And what else?"

"What do you mean, 'what else'? He works really hard. Plenty of reason to be exhausted. So what do you want for dinner? I can make a big salad, plus there's either lasagne or leftover Korean barbeque.. Any thoughts?" she said, bustling around, hands flying everywhere. Her hands were the best part of her. She was, in fact, an art teacher at the local community college, specializing in sculpture.

"My thoughts aren't about food."

"Well what are they about then? Don't be mysterious, Felice."

My ribs cinched together and I swallowed hard. What was I so afraid of? Isn't this just Mom in the kitchen?

I suddenly flashed on that gigantic pool at Corchoran Meadows Community Center. There I was, seven years old, standing on the edge of the high dive looking down at the water far, far below me. It was too much. I was terrified and promptly swiveled around to backtrack through the long line of kids on the ladder. It was the right decision then (although totally humiliating). And here I am nine years later, still better at swiveling than leaping.

"I've just got a lot going on, ensemble rehearsals, SAT redo, physics. I haven't even learned my music yet and our competition is in three weeks." Now I've just handed her the opportunity to roll out Polyanna again. Oh my God does she really think this will count as support? I guess the answer to that is yes.

If she puts her hand on my arm one more time, I will scream and our relationship will instantly vaporize.

She did and I flinched.

"Gotta go. See you later." I bolted.

Back to my green and lavender sanctuary. I lifted my violin out of its case, rosined the bow with extra vigor and flipped pages to Mozart's Quartet in G Major K387 on my music stand. I automatically placed the violin under my chin, with the bow poised for playing and stared at the music without recognizing any notes. Then I pivoted around, gently pitched my instrument onto the bed, laid down the bow and picked up my phone.

"Heyyo. I need to talk tonite before rehersal pls???? xox/fw"

"???? You OK? Can we chat after? I'm madly practicing... yikes. love you, yo"

"Not great but will survive. Till 6:30 then. f"

Ok. Funny how a tiny contact with the world beyond the family wall can allow you to breathe again.

I picked up my violin and began to play, stopping and starting at first, trying to find my focus, striving for the right notes, the right intonation, the proper rhythm, correctness being the mantra of my life. Slowly I began to feel myself climbing inside the next few measures, flirting with the dynamic changes, just for the sheer pleasure of it, for my ear, for my subtly swaying body, for the sake of my spirit yearning to rise. This music, which I approached with dread as just another "have-to," became a tonic for me in that moment. I soared inside it, then repeated it more fully, carving deeper valleys and higher peaks, all within a couple of minutes. But those 120 seconds opened for me a small window of possibilities of better feelings that were beyond imagining only a blink ago.

Practice time evaporated and I slipped out of the house without saying goodbye. I whipped open the backdoor of our gray Corolla and slung my violin case and bag in the back. Before checking the mirrors, I clipped my seatbelt and backed out of the driveway.

Carefully dodging the patches of frozen slush, I pulled into the school parking lot on the side by the music and theater building. And there was Yolanda, framed in the doorway, waving madly. I knew that underneath her blue wool hat was her serious-musician hairdo, i.e. a French braid. We one-arm-hugged so as not to bash our instruments together and forged ahead into rehearsal. So happy to see her.

The others were just arriving. Mack (on the cello), nordic beauty Hanna, viola, and Mr. Dietrich our fearless leader, also the head of Baxter High School's well-reputed music program. We (Yolanda and I) fondly referred to him as The Dour Mr. D. Which was funny to us, but possibly unfair. He must have found *some* things amusing somewhere.

Mack seated was just about as tall as Yolanda and I were standing. We were the raven-haired team and Mack and Hanna were the blondes. Black v. Blond. Mr. D.'s job was to bring us together somehow, with substantial help from Wolfgang Mozart, whose music appealed to us all.

We tossed our winter gear into piles and set about animating our fingers with our warm breath and various exercises. I was always amazed how breath stays so warm just a few membranes away from frigid air.

We tuned up. Mr. D. gave a hearty nose blow into his handkerchief, calling us to order. I was definitely not looking at Yolanda.

"We have a lot to cover tonight," Mr. D. began. "As you know, the competition is in three, yes, three weeks." He held up his fingers as if we needed some clarity. True, I thought, our last rehearsal was canceled due to snowstorms. Mr. D. went on: "I assume you all have been practicing non-stop at home." Silence. "Any questions before we begin? No? Well then, let's go, folks."

First violinist Yolanda dropped into a very focused place right away. To be fair, she was in her comfort zone and as out there as she could definitely be, there was a grounding she had access to, just like all the other members of her family, and that grounding was music. They celebrated this DNA link constantly, playing instruments and singing—even abuelita, her grandma (who I loved). Yolanda's family owned the only decent Mexican restaurant in town. On Saturday nights they formed a Mariachi band and entertained the happy customers aching for the tropics and a touch of the ethnic/exotic. But tonight here in this music room at Baxter High School I, too, had to somehow find my focus, with the competing distractions of my besieged brain and no known DNA to help me out.

Big breath. Okay. At least I can belong to the music.

Second violin lead into the finale and I played my part accurately. We were all mingling our musical threads together and I was beginning to float. "I can do this," I encouraged myself. "I *am* doing this, in spite of it all." And I played with more and more energy, pulling back on the soft parts, surging forward on the forte. I relished this experience, joining with others to make music, however imperfectly. My body followed my bow, dipping and rising, carving contours in the air, my right leg inching forward as I moved… making unplanned contact with my water bottle (the one with the mismatched top…which hit the floor rolling, pouring a river headed straight for Mr. D.'s briefcase propped gaping open on its side, poised for a drink.

Which it got.

The bottle was full.

The music stopped. I was horrified and went scrambling around with paper towels, repeating "Oh, I'm sorry. I am SO sorry." Mr. D. dumped his briefcase out in the sink and spread his sheets of music out to dry. There was a wet spot I had missed, but found it by skidding through on my way back to my chair. I settled back down in my seat, but the feelings I had been swallowing and the scene I had just created conspired together and shook me with laughter that I could not stop. My head was in my hands now wet with tears and my nose was running. Of course by this point the laughter had burst its container, too. Yolanda glared at me yelling, without saying one word, "Get a grip. What is WRONG with you??" But then she started in, too, and even Hanna and Mack got into it, all of us howling. Mr. D. just stood there waiting, half his face set in stone and the other half dawning with the slightest smile but for only a split second. He had no choice but to wait this one out so he set his lips on tight mode and flipped through the music.

An hour later—and by that I mean three minutes—I was sobering up, lagging slightly behind the others who were already zipped up and ready to focus.

"Ok, Ms. Model Minority. Are we ready now?"

My face burned.

But I got through it, as I always do. I show up. I function. I do reasonably well at violin and physics. What a complete picture I seem to be. Model minority. Was I proud, embarrassed or just pissed off?

I packed up at record speed, way ahead of Yolanda, who was taking her time. After Mack and Hanna exited, I approached Mr. D., not at all sure of what I wanted or needed to say.

"You want to apologize?" he guessed.

"I already did that."

"Question about Bar #106? Or do you want to know if you can bring your water bottle to the competition? The answer is yes, if it stays offstage in a far corner."

I was quiet and didn't feel like laughing pleasantly. He waited.

"Please don't ever say 'model minority' again."

"Felice—now you know it's meant as a compliment, acknowledging your success at Baxter High School."

Now I was stumped. Yeah, the language sounded good with the word 'model' and all.

I swear you could feel the heat rising from the other side of the room like the furnace had just kicked in.

"It is NOT a compliment," Yolanda fired from her corner. "Stereotyping is not a compliment. It's dehumanizing."

"WHOA," said Mr. D. in a state of mock shock, hand on his heart. "That's quite an overreaction, girls. It was meant as a compliment and you're completely misinterpreting. Anyway, I was just teasing. Don't be so SENSITIVE."

"Just promise you won't say it again," I managed.

"Fine. But if I slip, you'll have to forgive me and don't dwell. It's NOT a big deal."

"No, not to you," Yolanda said.

"Good night, girls." He all but pushed us through the door.

We hurried into the car. I turned to Yolanda.

"Thank you for saying what I was trying to say. You've got guts, girl."

"Well, you began the whole thing. I just followed up."

"Maybe…but your support means everything."

"Even if I'm not a proud member of the model minority?"

"Yeah. Even if."

I drove us to Yolanda's and called home to say when to expect me. We walked into the fragrant warmth of her home. Her grandma was in the kitchen making tamales to store in the freezer, always handy.

"Hola, abuelita," I sang out, even though she wasn't my official grandmother.

She reached up from the vantage point of four-foot-ten to my five-foot-one and embraced me. "Hola, querida."

Now *I* smelled like tamales but didn't mind at all. I have been soothed by the warm and bubbling energy of this family since Yolanda and I were in second grade. I felt a kinship with them that I could not clearly explain. They weren't remotely Korean. Yolanda wasn't adopted. Yet the gravitational pull was there for me.

"You came to visit me?" she said, twinkling and chuckling in her raspy way.

"Of course!" I said, falling happily into our predictable routine. "That's the only reason I gave Yolanda a ride home."

"Ah, bueno. Then sit down and wait for a nice tamale. Yolanda can go do her homework and we talk."

"Actually, I would love that, but I do have to talk with Yolanda and then dash home. Forgive me?"

"Okay, Felicia. But only if you promise me one thing."

"What would that be?"

"Bring home with you a tamale tonight."

"Well that's easy. Gracias, abuela."

Yolanda was waiting for me in the room she shared with her chatty ten year-old sister Cecilia, who, fortunately, was at a friend's house working on a science project. We had about 45 minutes. I closed the door and sat on the bright orange rug that lay between their two beds.

I eyed the glass of water near my elbow on the nightstand.

"Looking to recap that performance, are you?" Yolanda said.

"Yeah…that was so worth it. I haven't laughed that hard in forever."

We grinned with the freshness of that memory.

"So what's going on?" she asked.

"Lately I look in the mirror and it shocks me. It's like, oh my God, I'm not white. Does that ever happen to you?"

"Seriously? This is why you wanted to talk?? No. I never thought I was white…I guess your situation is a bit more confusing. But wait—did you think I was confused about you too?"

A cloud enveloped me. "Not really when you put it that way. I didn't actually put that together. Didn't even realize what I was thinking."

Yolanda just waited me out while words collected in my throat.

"I think my dad's dying. He has kidney disease and needs a donor, someone related to him, *by blood*. I found out by accident—it's apparently a secret." My voice broke open and by now I was sobbing. "I am so upset. I-I just can't lose him. He's been *my* lifeline. But, I can't be his."

Yolanda leaned forward and rested her hand on my arm. "Waitwaitwait. Back up a second. When and how did you find this out?"

I choked out the back story.

"So you haven't had any time to do research yet or talk with anyone? How do you know it's hopeless?"

"Obviously I don't know anything. Because no one tells me."

Yolanda gently shoved the tissue box in my direction. I lifted my head off my knees to reach for one as wet circles widened on top of each kneecap.

"Felice, are you saying you want to donate a kidney to your dad?"

Her question hung in the air and I inhaled it, holding it, warming it, for a moment longer.

My words tumbled all over each other in a hoarse, broken whisper. "Yeah—I would *so* love to do that. To be bonded with him in this very real way. It would be amazing."

"Plus, what a way to show your gratitude, right?"

"NOOO! Why is everyone so obsessed with gratitude? Even you! Wow. This is *not* about gratitude. I'm perfectly aware that I'm a lucky girl, that I could have perished in an orphanage without love or opportunity. C'mon, Yolanda. I don't need that speech now. PLEASE. This is about saving a life that I love. You're not adopted and you would want to do the same. And don't tell me that I should go talk with my parents. I'm not about to do *that*."

"Funny, that was my next piece of advice. So, anyway, what if you have the same blood type? What are the requirements for a donor anyway?"

"I don't know. I just assumed you have to be a blood relative. Which I think I finally get that I am *not*. In fact, I guess I'm not even the type of family member you can share information with."

"Can you stop being bitter for one minute and problem-solve with me? I can help you do some research. Maybe you can go to Community Health and find out your blood type. Contact your dad's estranged brother. There must be lots of options here. But of course, eventually, you'll have to deal with your parents directly, right?"

"You know, I hate you sometimes. You are so hyper-mature."

"Oh shut up."

"Seriously, Yo, you are the greatest friend. But I have to take care of this myself. And you can, if you like, be my highly paid consultant. I'm offering you a job."

She smiled, relieved, I'm sure, that I had stopped crying for the moment. 40 minutes had passed and I needed to gear myself up to go home for food, homework and plenty of awkwardness.

Abuelita was in the bathroom when I reached the front door. "Give her a hug goodbye for me," I said. "And here's one for you. Thanks again."

I strong-armed myself to concentrate on the drive home. "Blue pick-up ahead with brake lights on, stop sign partially obscured by shrub, signal to turn right," etc. until I finally pulled in the driveway and, of course, there, staring at me rudely, was the recycling bin. A big exhale on the cold windshield obscured the view just when I needed it.

I slipped past the room that was Dad's home office where I heard my parents' voices intently overlapping, straining to be quiet. Clutching my tamale, I quickly ducked into my room and closed the door. Computer on. I logged on to the Kidney Foundation and devoured the website for awhile, instead of the tamale.

After nearly an hour, drained and yawning over and over again, I got up out of my chair to stretch. The light was getting dim and my old first-grade glow-in-the-dark constellations were waking up on the ceiling. As I reached my arms up towards those plastic stars, I caught a glimpse of myself in the mirror: A hunk of totally straight hair hanging past my shoulders, pale tawny skin and wide cheekbones, eyes dark and slender. As I stared, trying to comprehend my own image, my imagination sketched in a frame of circles, circles that morphed into faces, Asian faces of all shapes and shadings, proliferating, nudging mine into the center. It was a surreal set of moments. I couldn't tear myself away from this odd vision of myself fitting in so seamlessly, in the center of any circle, instead of hovering on the edge. This was a possibility I had never considered before. Belonging was for other people like Yolanda, something I didn't want to think about. Or feel about.

I shut my eyes and turned away from the mirror. There was a stack of blank strips of paper on my desk, beckoning. These days I fed my envelopes with questions that simmered, rather than with the narrative of a child's life straining to be perfect. I noticed the word "longing" wedged inside the word "belonging," like it dominated it completely. I reached for a pen.

Where is my place of belonging? Why do I even care?
What is bonding?
What is family?
How did my life begin and who does it belong to?
What does fate have to do with anything?
Isn't there a flip side to lucky? Can I say that out loud?

My hand and my pen slowly, carefully guided these questions out of my brain. I sealed each paper strip in its own white envelope—private, protected—questions alone and unanswered.

Actually, there was one more blank strip of paper left in front of me for one extra question. But not "What is friendship?" That one I already understood.

Text buzz:
"how's the research?
       "Pretty okay—going to community health clinic tomorrow for blood test."
"awesome. cheers from sidelines."
       "Thx...grateful for your s'port...luv you."

New buzz:
"Where r u?" (It was mom, trying to be a hipster texter.)
       "In my room working."
"Didn't hear u come in. Hungry?"
       "Not really. I ate before."
"can I come in? I'm outside your door."
       "Not right now please...zzzz. See you tomorrow. Luv you."
"worried bout u. luv u 2. g'nite"
       "luv u + dad too".
       xox

I watched her shadow shrink from the underedge of the door as she retreated, in the interest of being the perfectly supportive mom. Well, why not? Perfect moms breed perfect daughters. Or *not* breed in this case.

I swiftly cleared my room: Boxes back in the closet, computer logged off, lights out. Tiredness totally ambushed me and I literally fell into bed. Despite my churning brain, I managed to finally conk out. And although I slept, dreams robbed me of rest.

I woke up before the alarm, shaky and exhausted. I took off for school in a blind rush. Once I had exited the house, I realized my bedroom door might not have been closed tight, but I figured that at this point, it was better to keep going than to re-enter.

• • •

The morning crawled by till it was finally lunchtime. We were allowed to go off-campus during our 48-minute hour so I blitzed down the block to the Community Health Center and strode quickly across the beige speckled linoleum to the reception desk. My eyes darted around like a fugitive. Natalie, the thirty-something spiky-haired woman behind the desk, smiled at me mechanically and waited for me to say something.

"I need to know my blood type."

"Ok, sure. Insurance or ca—?"

"Cash," I blurted. This was my very first experience feeling empathy for bank robbers.

I paid and sat down with the clipboard she handed me. I filled out my medical history quickly. When you're adopted you get to skip a lot of questions.

Reason for test…this was legally confidential, right? I wrote "qualifying for organ donation." And handed it back to Natalie. She did not even blink one time.

I was ushered back to the lab and was promptly saturated with the smell of alcohol and the sight of tubes of blood and packages of needles, bearing down on my senses without mercy. I focused on the pictures of the kitty cats on the wall peeking out of baskets and gift-wrapped packages, but the sting of the needle brought on a wave of nausea.

"Doin' great!" chirped the technician.

She was wrong. I could feel the color draining out of me and I was sure I'd finally morphed into that white person I used to believe I was. Then she loosened the tourniquet and I was free.

"Results in by the end of the week," she said.

• • •

Still not feeling too stable, I grabbed the blueberry yogurt stashed in my backpack and sat down in the reception area. There were questions dragging on me and I didn't feel ready to go back to school and cram my brain full of Algebra 3.

So what if I did qualify? What pain would I go through to sacrifice (I mean donate) a kidney? What would the rest of my life be like? Could I run, ski, tour with an orchestra? What is dad going through right now? Is he in pain? Is he scared? Will he win this race against time? Someday all too soon this would all come to a head.

I stepped out into the frigid air and emptied my lungs. Even my thick scarf (ingeniously made from recycled plastic bottles) did not quiet the shivering layers below the surface of my skin. I headed back to the overheated classrooms of Baxter.

3:30 and I was the first one home. Snatched an apple from the fruit drawer and hustled off to my room. The door was ajar and it was a total mess, but not the normal total mess. Blank envelopes were strewn on the floor near my closet, some open, some mangled. That membrane between polite and angry began to disintegrate. I snatched the phone.

"Hi honey. Is everything ok?"

"NO. Definitely NOT ok. Why were you going through my stuff? It's PRIVATE!"

"What in the *world* are you talking about? I have no idea what you are talking about, Felice. No one has gone through your stuff."

"My boxes...the envelopes were all over the floor. Some were opened, some were crumpled. It's NONE OF YOUR BUSINESS!"

"I'll be home in ten minutes and we'll talk."

. . .

I clicked off and threw the phone on the bed. Claws scratched the rug under the bed as a certain dog was roused from her nap. I lifted the edge of the bedspread and saw Miya there with a tidbit of paper hanging from her lower lip. A tidbit with my handwriting on it.

"Oh... guess it was *you*," I said out loud, remembering that she had a taste for paper. Uhhh...I probably hadn't closed the door all the way when I bolted this morning.

I patted Miya on the head and removed the evidence from her mouth. I had to admit that seeing that little dogface softened my heart and I knelt down to kiss her on the muzzle. Maybe there was a trace of tamale on my fingers when I last handled this box. And that would have rendered her helpless in the face of temptation. Mom walked in with her jacket still zipped, bags in hand. Before she could speak, I said, "Mom, I'm really sorry. It was Miya. I'm sorry I jumped on you like that."

"Uh...okaay," she said slowly, carefully. "So what's going on, Felice? You're not exactly your sunny self lately."

I had that feeling again, of one foot dangling off the edge of the high dive. It was so tempting to step off this time, step off and sail triumphantly through the air before slipping silently into the water.

I caught a glimpse of her lips cemented together and the color of her eyes gone matte-finish. My windpipe shrunk into what felt like a narrow straw. What if she blew me off (in a nice way, of course—which I hate more than anything)? Then would I be able to maintain calm? I had zero confidence in that.

So I took one giant step back from the edge.

"I have a lot on my mind," I said, pretending to look through the papers on my bed as I could sense her gaze following me. "I'll talk to you soon, I promise."

"Ok. Any time." She turned to leave, still holding her bags and turned around at the door. "We love you, you know."

"Yeah, me too…Oh, you remember I'm going back to school from six to eight to help hang work for the junior/senior art exhibit. I'll be home by 8:15."

"All right. Thanks for the reminder," she said and quietly left.

I smoothed out the crumpled envelopes and returned them to the box. Then I laid down on my bed with my physics textbook to see if I could pull my mind into a different unreal world than the one I was occupying here in the state of Colorado. This worked well for about 90 minutes. Then I left for BHS.

As it turned out, a ton of kids came to help set up the art exhibit. The creative types at our school are a relatively small crowd, but we leap at any excuse for togetherness and here was a good one. Party for a higher purpose.

I placed my own work, an acrylic/collage piece titled "Finding the Thread" in which a thin green string appears, disappears and reappears throughout the painting. I actually had no idea what this was about when I created it last fall; it just flowed onto the paper as I worked the design elements. But now I could see that this was a portrait of the life I was living boxed up in my closet.

After helping set up a few 3-D pieces, I figured there were more than enough volunteers and headed out. It was early, but you only have to call home when you're late.

• • •

When I got home, I left my wet shoes at the door and padded up the stairs. The door of my room was closed, but the light was on. I didn't think I had left the light on. I opened the door quietly and was stunned to see my mom sitting on my bed strewn with envelopes. Opened envelopes.

"WHAT are you doing?? I can't believe this," I yelled at point blank range. "You have NO right!"

"I was worried," she stammered. "I...I thought you were in trouble. Maybe you were hiding something that we ought to know about. It was for your own protection, Felice. You must understand that's what caring parents..."

"Well, I don't need your phony protection! This is *NONE* of your business. Give me those! Can you just leave now?? I will *never* trust you again. JUST LEAVE!"

She was ashen. "This time I'm not leaving," she said in a near-whisper, "until you talk to me."

I slammed my bag against the wall and glared through the window with the pastel curtains.

She stepped into our silence, pleading. "We are your family. You are our daughter, Felice, and we love you more than anything."

"I'm not and you don't."

She leaned her head into her hands as I've never seen her do. I saw her shoulders trembling and knew she was crying. I tried my best to look at her with contempt, to hang on to my new cruelty. But then she said, "Oh, yes, you *are* our family. You know, giving birth doesn't automatically make someone a mother."

"Yeah?? Well, how about this: Giving up your baby for adoption doesn't make someone less of a mother either."

"All right, Felice. All right. Fair enough. Calm down." She drew the back of her hand across her cheeks. "It's just that...we love you more than you know. And I don't know why you don't know. I don't know why, but what I've just read tells me that, after all this time, you don't get it and I don't understand. I just don't understand and it breaks my heart," she sobbed.

By then I was crying, too. "Why didn't you tell me about dad if you wanted me to feel so much like part of the family? If I *really* belong, then why did I have to find out by accident from the letter you threw away? It just made everything I've been feeling all along pretty clear. I'm on the outside of this little circle."

"Is *that* what this is about?"

"Not totally. It's more about my entire life."

"What on earth does that mean? You never mentioned this before."

"Just because I haven't talked about it doesn't mean I'm not thinking about it," I bellowed. "I've always felt like a pretender, pretending to be happy-smiley-talented-lucky-WHITE...and a true member of this whole big family. Here I am, sweating my brains out to fulfill your daughterdreams and I'm actually a fake. Can't you see that?"

"But we never asked that you be anything other than what you are and want to be. We took you to Culture Camp and celebrated Korean Christmas when you were little. We encouraged you to choose a Korean name for your puppy and made Korean treats for your eighth birthday party. How is that denying who you are and where you came from? It sounds like affirmation to me. You know, there are lots of parents who would never have even bothered..."

"That was all for you, not me. So you could convince yourselves and the rest of the world that you were A+ parents."

The floodgates were open now and I barreled on:

"You just don't get it. Why didn't YOU talk about these things with me, asking me how *I* felt, what was going on in my heart about being in this family, in this country? But you didn't, so it was like a taboo subject. And now that I've finally explained, you still don't see me. I'm just floating on a raft in the middle of the ocean and you think I'm walking on land in Colorado. I don't belong *anywhere* and least of all to you."

At that point, she squeezed her eyes shut pushing more tears down her cheeks. I hated watching this, witnessing her stress. Her shoulders heaved and she exhaled with some force, trying hard to collect herself.

"Wow...you've never said any of these things before. I really wish you had. If I had known you needed to talk, I would have been there. I was just taking what I thought was your lead, waiting, wanting to respect your privacy. I guess I misunderstood. I...I'm so sorry," she said, her voice fragmenting again. Despite my best efforts to wall her off, I started to sense her compassion.

She sighed and somehow altered the airspace in my room.

"So where do we go from here, Felice? Your dad needs a new kidney. We didn't want you to worry or to anguish over providing it. Even if you were related biologically, we wouldn't allow you to be the donor."

"It actually *is* what I want to do. And I can't. Do you know how that feels?"

"Yes, I think I do," she said. "Maybe you can let yourself imagine how much I, too, wanted to do the same thing. But I don't qualify either. I don't think I've ever been so disappointed."

I said nothing. My fingers raked Miya's fur over and over making deep tracks appear.

The door opened so silently behind me that I heard nothing, until a deep, gentle voice said, "I have four things to say: First of all, I'm going to be ok waiting for a donor. Second, thank you, Felice, for trusting us as much as you do to say as much as you have. Third, I love you both with all my heart. And finally," he said hoarsely, "I have never felt so loved in my whole life as I have listening to the two of you from the other side of this door. And I am so grateful."

At this point, the three of us became a sodden mass, tears running everywhere, yet each still in the embrace of our own private suffering. But my unanswered questions pushed me forward and I was the first to speak, softly:

"Just tell me the truth, please. I need to know what's going on."

Mom waited, looking down at her hands with the crumpled tissue. My eyes rested on dad's face and I noticed the tiredness that had accumulated around his gray-blue eyes, the color that had escaped from his usual ruddy skin, his jowls that were beginning to hang lower. I didn't know whether these changes happened all at once when I had my back turned or right in front of me when I simply wasn't paying attention. But now I was fully awake. He cleared his throat and began to speak solemnly.

"I have what they call Stage three kidney disease."

I interrupted, "How long have you known this?"

"Only a few weeks, Felice. I noticed my symptoms were getting worse. I felt more and more tired and haven't been very interested in food. So I went in for some tests and they indicated a declining kidney function. I'm a good candidate for a transplant because my overall health is ok... "

"Yeah, except for the kidney disease."

"Right... Leesie." Hearing my somewhat ridiculous nickname and especially seeing his faintly lopsided grin calmed me down, tilted me toward believing that things were almost back to normal, whatever that was. "But although I qualify, I'm not the one in the most dire need, so the letter you saw was about that. I'm so sorry you had to find out that way."

"The truth is I did not *have* to find out that way."

"Ok, you're right. But please understand, we didn't want you to worry or be distracted from your friends and your school work and all your activities for something you can't do anything about. In no way were we trying to push you out or hurt you."

"Well, you *did*."

"Did you hear me say I'm sorry? That's all I can do."

"I want to call Uncle Brian," I blurted out.

And that killed the conversation.

Uncle Brian is my dad's estranged twin brother who I kind of liked but haven't seen since I was five. It was then that he "disappeared" from us, mysteriously eliminated from family events and family talk. When I was older, around eight, I peppered them with questions about him. At first they were evasive and so I went underground with my wondering, some of it buried in the envelopes in my closet where I created stories about his disappearance.

But later mom explained that Uncle Brian was a strong opponent of international adoption and freely shared his opinions. In fact, he ranted at my dad that adopting me was more than just a selfish act on their part, but also unethical, to rob a child of their birth culture and participate in the international adoption "industry." My parents could not absorb this viewpoint and were worried it would eventually have a negative impact on me. So in their mild but firm way, they invited him to leave and POOF! he was gone, never to return.

"No. That will not happen."

My mother chimed in, "We've already discussed this, Felice. Your dad is dead set against it."

"Weird that you said 'dead set'. What if he is the only donor who can save his life?"

"There are other donors around. We'll find one. It takes time and I have time. Still got 48% of my function left and I'm on a special diet now that should help protect my kidneys."

"This makes *no* sense! How could less than 50% be a good thing??"

"Please stop, Felice," my mother said looking at me gently, pushing a stray curl off her own forehead. "This is for us to handle.

It's not in your lap, even if you have the information now and you understand. We're still the adults here."

Dad looked so exhausted that I was willing to cut off this piece of conversation so he could lie down.

"I'm going to take a rest now." He reached over and pulled me to him with one arm. I wrapped my arms around him and laid my ear on his chest till I could hear his heart beating steadily.

"I love you, Dad."

"Me too, sweetheart."

On her way out the door, mom lightly smoothed my hair and left the room.

I leaned my back against the door, my head off-angle to one side. It was just too demanding to keep it vertical. Or to think, for that matter. A sort-of calm (or exhaustion) came over me and I wanted to surrender to it. But first I had to quickly reorganize my pilfered writings for their protection and my comfort. Vowing to myself that I would only spend a few efficient minutes doing this—a vow I was very familiar with and had broken many times—I nonetheless plucked out an envelope from Box #4, sixth grade:

"My birthday! The iPod I've been saving for!! (mom and dad paid the rest)

"Here's the card: (all different shades of green)

"I wonder if there is someone else who thinks of me every year on this day?"

• • •

I read and re-read this line and let the question linger. Then I carefully put it away and went on to Box #8, just one year ago. Things were starting to get pithier.

"Home from Youth Symphony Spring Concert and MY SOLO. Got a standing O. Parents were ecstatic, couldn't stop saying how proud they were. For me, more of an anti-climax. I don't know why.

You'd think they would notice but..."

. . .

I shut my eyes and slumped against the closet wall. In my imagination, a face like mine, round with delicate features, belonging to a woman I knew for only nine months, wondering, searching for some peace and acceptance in the excruciating absence of information. Like me. Maybe we're in this together? But I couldn't hold on. My imagination suddenly imploded and she dissolved for the umpteenth time.

I just can't keep losing parents.

I thought about Uncle Brian. It doesn't matter to me what his opinions were or are about international adoption. I made no promises about him today...except the one I was now making to myself.

Brian Woodson was actually not hard to find. Still lived in the same town, same house, an hour away. The challenge was now finding the right alibi.

Yolanda.

I phoned.

"Do you realize what time it is??"

"No, what time is it? Oh my God, I'm so sorry. I had no idea it was already midnight."

"Can this be quick? I gotta get some sleep."

"Yeah, ok, I'll be brief. Big explosion with my parents. Things are ok. Going to hunt for Uncle Brian. Need your help. Talk to you tomorrow. Sweet dreams."

"Whoa," she said so softly and sleepily that I wondered if she would remember any of this in the morning. But it was enough for now and I hung up. The brief shot of adrenalin was wearing off and my own deep fatigue began to overpower me.

I woke up Saturday around 10:00. There was a note on the kitchen table—"Out walking Miya." Mail was scattered on the floor underneath the mail slot by the front door and one envelope had my name on it. Return address: Community Health Center. "Confidential" I ripped it open and read: Blood Type A-. Well, that confirmed my unsuitability: Dad was B+. Time to confront my estranged uncle. I scribbled a note under theirs about hanging out with Yolanda till the afternoon and headed out.

She was ready and we headed down Route 45 to our neighboring town. 1940 West 3rd Ave. No music. No conversation.

I finally intruded on our quiet with the obvious confession: "I'm nervous."

"Me too, and it's not even about me or my dad," Yolanda yawned. "What are you going to say?"

"I'll ask if I can come in and talk," I said not feeling all that inspired. I pushed a hunk of hair under my red wool hat, three times until I got all strands stuffed in. "That's all I've planned so far..."

"So what's the worst that can happen?"

"He slams the door in my face. Or he calls my parents and screams at them for putting me on the front line to contact him instead of my dad."

"The first is more likely than the second. But I don't think either will happen, actually. Tell him right away that they do not know you are here, that it was your decision alone to seek him out."

"He could still slam the door. And that would totally kill me."

"It would kill you more not to try. Here, have an ice cold breakfast burrito."

"Thanks, Yo. Not only did you agree to come with me, but you even brought a picnic."

The burrito sat in my stomach like ground glass.

The streets were lined with split-level wood frame houses, designed in one of two ways, split on the left or split on the right, in pale green, yellow or blue. The saving grace was that the avenues were laid out in a grid pattern and there was no mistaking where West 3rd was. We parked across the street, slightly west of 1940 and waited. The driveway was empty, the garage door shut.

I gulped my water too fast and some slipped into my windpipe, setting off a coughing fit. My phone buzzed with a text from my mom, something about pesto chicken pizza for dinner, Yolanda welcome. Back to her usual pleasantly helpful way of "connecting" with me. Texted back "Sure."

• • •

We sat there staring out the windshield, hypnotized by cascades of snowflakes floating down from a place beyond my fathoming. We waited and watched the snow collect silently on the windows, sealing us off from the outside into another world, neutral and uncomplicated. Like the world I longed for more every day.

But suddenly I needed to breathe different air. I threw the door open without warning. Yolanda cranked her head so quickly in my direction that she grabbed her neck in pain. The door shut with a muffled sound, sending one layer of snow to the pavement. I planted my boot deliberately to mark my presence and then paused for a split second to admire the perfect clarity of that footprint, as if it were a work of art that had required thought, planning and know-how. I leaned into the flurry of flakes and headed for the house.

Two hours later we reached home again, no questions asked, no frantic texts. I dropped Yolanda at her door.

"Thanks SO much for being there," I said. "You gave me more than the breakfast burrito, you know. Like courage."

"Yeah," she said. "It was a good thing. Let's catch up later, ok? Gotta run."

I waved her out and drove home feeling a strange steadiness. No one seemed to be home, which was actually just what I needed. On my bed was a blank envelope which was definitely not one of mine. No trauma signals blaring, just plain old curiosity, led me to carefully open the envelope and extract the pale blue sheet of paper with a message framed in a scatter of red flowers, delicately penned by my mother, signed by both of them.

> *Dear Felice,*
> *Keep searching. Keep asking. Keep expressing.*
> *And all the while, please remember that we hope someday*
> *you will feel as connected to us as we do so deeply to you.*
> *We're here and we love you.*
> *Mom and Dad*

The note sat in my lap for a minute and stared up at me. They couldn't know what I was up to, right? I wasn't sure how to respond, especially in light of today's events. I folded the blue paper slowly in on itself with a single new crease, then tucked it away behind Box #8.

END NOTES

5   "The Primal Wound" by Nancy Newton Verrier, Gateway Press, April 1, 1993.

6   Katie Agranat, Adoptees for Positivity blog, date unknown, no longer posted.

7   "Interpolated Spheres," YouTube interview with adoptee artists Christina Seong, Nari Baker, Darius Morrison, November 28, 2012.

8   "PBS Made Me Cry," Keum Mee, Land of Gazillion Adoptees blog, October 18, 2012 (originally appeared in *Adoption Constellation Magazine*, published by Adoption Mosaic).

9   T.R.I.A. (Transracial International Adoptee) therapists. See Resource section for guidance in choosing an adoption-competent therapist (who may or may not be TRIA).

10 "Korean Looks, American Eyes: Korean American Adoptees, Race, Culture and Nation" by Kim Ja Park Nelson, University of Minnesota, Department of American Studies, December, 2009.

11 Eun Mi, "Cultures of Transnational Adoption," Toby Alice Volkman, editor, Duke University Press, June 2005.

12 Amy Lee Scott, Land of Gazillion Adoptees interview, October 16, 2012.

13 Isabella Rossellini, "Cultures of Transnational Adoption," Toby Alice Volkman, editor, Duke University Press, June 2005

PICK UP YOUR PEN

The rest of the story is in your hands. Here are some questions to consider:

1. What are your hopes for Felice at this point?

_____

_____

_____

_____

_____

_____

2. How would you like the story to resolve?

_____

_____

_____

_____

_____

_____

3. What aspects of belonging are you looking for?
   (biological, kinship, emotional understanding, shared
   experience and interests)

_____

_____

_____

_____

_____

_____

_____

4. What kinship group is most important to you right now, the one where you feel the greatest sense of belonging? What can you do to further enrich these connections?

_____

_____

_____

_____

_____

_____

5. How do you create a bond with those who are different than you? Are common interests and values enough to give you what you need in terms of connection with friends, co-workers and community?

_____

_____

_____

_____

_____

_____

6. How does race or country of origin affect your sense of connection? Do you want or seek friendships with others from your background? How important is it for you that they are also adoptees? International adoptees, specifically?

_____

_____

_____

_____

_____

_____

7. How has your family supported or hindered you in the process of connecting with your heritage, including your birth family? What would you have done differently as a parent?

_____

_____

_____

_____

_____

_____

_____

8. What impact do you think it might have for your sense of belonging to connect with your birth culture, visit your homeland or birth family, or meet other adoptees?

_____

_____

_____

_____

_____

_____

9. How can you go about belonging to your own story?

_____

_____

_____

_____

_____

_____

_____

Ni Hao Ma

by Stephen Johnson

What if I told you...
That not all Asians are Chinese.

And hear me out,
There's nothing wrong with being Chinese.

It's just that...
I'm not.

You see, it's really hard for me
To be Chinese
When I'm already Korean.

So, the other day
I was in line at the bookstore
And I heard the foreign yet familiar
Words from a friendly female behind me

Ni hao ma!

The words rattled in my head before I realized
    what was happening
Like a shock to my senses or a splash of water to my face
And I just stared straight ahead

Ni hao ma?

The words came again
This time with a twinge of a question
Like the speaker was somehow second guessing herself
All the similar moments rushed through my head
The micro-aggressions and internal suppressions
Years of isolation and castration
The expectation for me to be
Something that I'm not

And I wanted to scream
And so I turned to her
 Smiling politely and said,
"Sorry, but I'm Korean"
And my feet took me traversing towards an exit
Apologizing as if I was wrong by my own existence

You see, I like to imagine myself as a beacon of normative
    behavior
A savior for the haters and traitors
But the truth is
In the heat of the moment
I often don't know what to say
And so I retreat to my room
And write poetry
Imagining all the things I'd like to say

In that moment I wanted to round up all of Asian America
To show that we are more than oriental objects
For you to propitiate and propagate
An agenda built upon the backs of servants and slaves
Your shining stars to show how bootstraps can be
    pulled up properly,
a property for your monopoly.

I wanted to tell her about dynasties and comfort women
Displaced lives and internment prisons
Visions of millions of immigrant decisions
We are more than laundromats and funny fats
Tattoos on frat dudes
More than fried rice and slanted eyes
Mulan and Ching Chang Chong
And I wanted to call upon all the adoptees I know
And rain down with the full force of our diversity

To show her that we are not what you think
I wanted to sit down
To share coffee and spill education
To tell her that I can't drive
But it's not because I'm Asian

We are more than a model for other minorities
Shit, we are a model for everyone

We are narratives and ancestors
We are loss and reconnection
We are displaced and disaffected
We are people
Complex, happy and savvy
Like Glenn is to Maggie
A collection of intersections
The reflection of a new direction
And just because you can't pronounce our family names
Doesn't mean we all look the same

And I've been called some terrible things in my life
Chink, Jap, Charlie

To name the pain reclaims the shame
But the funny thing is that race isn't a thing
A social construct to calculate our conduct
Based upon the color of our skin

And yet it feels like the most powerful thing in the world
The fact that somehow people are more valuable than others
Based on specimens of melanin
And yet we wear privilege like an apron
Draped to our napes like Paula Dean is to bacon
And I'm tired of mistaking and faking
As if I'm not just as guilty

As everyone else in the room
Because if silence is approval
Then my lack of words is an oppression
A digression from the progressive lessons
We never seem to learn

It's like me walking up to a Russian
And saying *Bonjour, wi wi monsieur*
And she would look at me
With the absurdity of societies and proprieties
Being lumped into the melting pot
Of our so-called American Dream
Where to assimilate
Means we must give up all of our identities
And that is the best part of me
America, you are missing out
On the best part of me

And it's not just us of the Asian persuasion
If you're Latina, you're nothing more than an illegal alien
AFRICA IS NOT A COUNTRY.
It's a continent with complex cultures
And let me be the first to tell you
That not all black men are out to get you
Your innocent ignorance sends us to therapists
And how did Sikh's somehow become terrorists?

And yet life is more complicated
And the only way to change the world is to let your stories
breathe free

Ni hao ma!

Race, Culture, Ethnicity

MY SKIN IS NOT ME

...My skin color is not
The content of my character,
Being black
Does not decide my heart.
Being brown
Does not make up my mind.
Being white
Does not determine who I am
inside.
To know me
You have to learn me...[14]

IT'S NOT TOO MUCH TO ASK. To be seen for who we are and how we wish to be seen, beyond the jumble of labels and mislabels into the fullness of our complexity.

We humans seem to have a penchant for organizing people into groups and categories, our default temptation in this often-chaotic world. But grasping for labels—whether for ourselves or others—can be a dangerous business, and pretty much guarantees that much will be overlooked.

267,098.

That is the number of international adoptees—mostly babies and children of color—who joined predominantly white American families between 1999 and 2016. While transnational adoptions to the U.S. have plummeted 77% since the peak year of 2004, the U.S. continues to be the country that adopts internationally more than any other—the largest number of children coming from China.[15]

As an adoptee whose life began in another country, odds are overwhelming that you are a person of color who joined a white family. In fact, 84% of international adoptees in the U.S. are racially different than their adoptive families.[16] This situation ups the challenge of discovering and inhabiting your racial and ethnic identities—which are essential pieces of rising self-esteem. It is no wonder that most of those interviewed for this project, as well as many others who have written about their experiences as international adoptees, say that finding positive racial and ethnic identity has been a driving issue in their lives from childhood onward.

Some adoptive parents might find this to be a surprising piece of news. They may have made a sincere effort to be supportive by providing opportunities like culture camp, making a special effort to include foods from their child's birth country, special books, or have even supported homeland travel. Yet while these have become more common practices for adoptive families in recent years, there are still some adoptive parents who would rather pretend that everyone in the family is white—and ethnically identical—as a way of attempting to create a sense of "inclusion." The challenges of being a child of color in a white family, as well as the complexities of parenting this child, often go unrecognized.

Regardless of which approach is taken, there is no sidestepping the subject of racial and ethnic difference in such families. Wherever these words take you, and however you define them (out loud or not), there they are, smack in the middle.

Truly, some of the most important early conversations about race and ethnicity begin within the family. They shape how we feel about ourselves, our expectations of others, and how we deal with the challenges of prejudice and racism. Yet all too often the sidestepping happens. While issues of race and ethnicity hover, some people turn away from them—or else treat them so lightly as to make them seem unimportant. As a result, misunderstandings and feelings of isolation arise. Meanwhile, the impacts of racial and cultural differences continue to be the lived experience—some would say on a daily basis—for most international adoptees in America.

So, is race real, or is it a concoction? And does it really matter?[17]

There is room to wonder about such questions, at least at an academic level. Whatever your personal opinion on that may be, if you are an adoptee of color, your life experience probably tells you that society treats race as a real thing. That has consequences: Positive, negative, and sometimes confusing. So maybe race is technically a real thing or maybe it's not. But your *experience* of it is certainly real.

You've undoubtedly noticed that many people feel a need to pigeonhole your racial and ethnic identity. But that doesn't mean they get to define you with their ideas, stereotypes or otherwise. Defining yourself is *your* journey, not theirs.

Whether it is at the top of your list or not, these issues are hanging around, waiting to be dealt with. While some adoptees are not at all interested in how racial or cultural identities have played out in their lives—indifference to these topics is not necessarily ideal for the long haul. In reality, these issues are embedded in each adoptee's journey of self-discovery and affirmation.

GROWING UP IN WHITENESS

"I was *the diversity in my high school."—Anonymous*

Some adoptees argue that they had an advantage being children of color raised in white communities where they learned firsthand to be familiar and relatively comfortable with white people. This is an interesting point, but I believe it is outweighed by the inherent disadvantages hinted at by the international adoptee quoted above, who remembers with irony that she nearly single-handedly brought diversity to her high school.

One possible implication of her statement is that minority kids who growing up in predominantly white environments find it *more* difficult to feel comfortable in diverse environments which include those people they can identify with—racially, culturally, and ethnically. Understandably, most adoptees interviewed touted the importance of growing up in diverse communities, whether they themselves had experienced this personally or vicariously through adopted friends.

Our family resided in a "progressive" community. We naively thought that our daughter would benefit from the open attitudes combined with the smattering of diversity, that she would likely avoid being the target of racism in this environment. No doubt this expectation was influenced by the lens through which we perceived the world, a lens tinted white. It turned out that despite all our conscious efforts to connect our daughter with her heritage and the beauty of our multicultural world, we were not able to shield her from the challenges she, as a person of color, faced in our "enlightened" town. But thanks in part to relocating to a much more diverse community years ago, she has emerged with a sturdy pride in her multi-faceted identity and a healthy radar for negative messaging. This was greatly enhanced by connections with those who understood all these issues from the inside out.

≈

"Race was a non-issue because I made it so. But by whitewashing every aspect of my life, I missed out on potentially enriching experiences that would have deepened my understanding of the racial plurality that was my existence. At college I met fellow Token Asians. When we compared notes from growing up, I realized that I wasn't a total freak after all." —AMY LEE SCOTT[18]

≈

"After growing up in a white rural area, going to college was a diversity shock." —SELENA

≈

"One of the most damaging experiences for me personally as a transracial, intercountry adoptee was growing up completely isolated within a predominantly White community. All my parents' friends were White. All my White siblings' friends were White. The neighborhoods we lived in were White. The schools we attended were majority White (with a few token minorities here and there).

"And the ironic thing is that my adoptive family lived in Asian countries for a good part of my childhood. So, it wasn't that I never saw other Asian people. It was that my parents never made an effort to make Asian people and culture a part of our family and lives.

"Rather, full assimilation within the Whiteness was what was thought to be best." —MILA KONOMOS[19]

≈

And if that's the main message, it can push you to meet a false standard and reject yourself in the process—if you happen to be other than a white person.

CRAVING WHITENESS:
INTERNALIZED RACISM

In a study of international adoptees by the Evan B. Donaldson Adoption Institute conducted in 2009, 78% of the adult respondents remembered wanting to be white as children.[20]

❧

"Sometimes it still sounds so trite, so trivial when I try to explain it now. Almost all the girls in my class had blond hair and blue eyes. I heard chink and Chinee on the playground at least once a week, from second through eighth grades, usually accompanied by pulled-back eyes and taunts in a sing-song, fake-accented voice. Until the age of nine, when we hosted two Japanese exchange students for a single weekend, I never spent any time with anyone who looked anything like me. I always felt anxious, exposed, like everyone was staring at me...If I'd been granted a magic wish, I would have chosen to be white in a heartbeat." —NICOLE SOOJUNG CALLAHAN [21]

❧

Another adoptee expressed doubts that her parents were aware of how much she struggled with her identity. "They never asked," she says. "Race in our houschold was never discussed. Because there weren't many Asians in the community I grew up in, I always felt like I had some deficit because I wasn't white."

❧

"And as a transracial adoptee, I can say without hesitation, that growing up in a White family that was oblivious and ignorant to racial issues and identity was damaging to the core of who I am. I'm approaching my 40's, and I still struggle with feeling like my race is a defect or is somehow less desirable, less beautiful, less meaningful than being White." —MILA KONOMOS [22]

Maybe you, too, once believed that somehow you should have been white after years of absorbing messages from those in your immediate environment—as well as the media. After years of soaking in this bias—whether directly, or in a more insidious way—you might actually find yourself not truly seeing your own reflection in the mirror. Or not wanting to.

～

"I spent a good piece of my life in envy of that blond hair and, especially, those blue eyes. Even though I do not remember a time when I did not know I was adopted from Korea, I do remember a long period of time when I was raised to forget that I was from Korea; to believe that I was the same as everyone else around me..."
– SHELISE GIESEKE[23]

～

Turning in on yourself and rejecting your own origins might seem like a necessary step toward being accepted into white society. But that's a high price to pay.

"...Sometimes, I like to describe my need to assimilate as a drug: It was an addiction that blinded me from every aspect of who I was. It was as if I injected whiteness into my veins and allowed it to take over my thoughts and actions. I convinced myself that if I acted like I was part of the dominant, mainstream body and mind, then I could convince everyone else that I was too.

"I remember distinct moments in time when I literally thought I was white. In kindergarten, I confidently told my class I was German because my last name is German. In high school, I lectured one of my teachers about how Asian-American culture wasn't important to me because I saw myself as white... I actually formulated the idea that I would socially benefit by ignoring who I truly was. I completely made myself believe that whiteness equated to happiness.

"...Despite telling myself and others that I was white, my outward appearance was still clearly Asian. My skin color made me subject to a lot of racist bullying while growing up. I couldn't escape the daily microaggressions and overt racism, so eventually I began to internalize it all by picking up the 'If you can't beat them, you might as well join them' mindset. I started winning approval of others by making 'funny' racist jokes toward myself. I even took on the nicknames 'Wonton' and 'Egg Roll.' The more I did it, the more people thought that I was funny and seemed to like me...but for all the wrong reasons." —ERICA GEHRINGER [24]

~

"Though my parents encouraged me to attend Korean school, I refused because it seemed way too weird. Still, I reveled in being the token Asian in my white community, but essentially ignored everything about my biological roots. I avoided Asia and kids at school for fear of being labeled as one of them—FOB math whizzes who ate stinky seaweed at lunch. Even as a kid, I could stereotype like nobody's business." —AMY LEE SCOTT [25]

COLORBLIND/CULTUREBLIND

Here's a story from an adult Asian adoptee raised in a white American family of Norwegian descent, who once attended a neighborhood party with her white fiancé. When they had a chance to talk alone afterward he expressed bewilderment that someone had approached him at the party to say how happy she was to have another mixed-race couple in the neighborhood. "I didn't have a clue what she was talking about," the white fiancé said. "I mean, I'm Irish and you're Norwegian."

In another instance, a white parent insisted that he was Asian like his young adopted daughter. Although he was unambiguously Caucasian, he rationalized that since all humans originate from the same genetic root, *technically* there was no such thing as racial difference. A unique approach to race-blindness to be sure, but one that was undoubtedly confusing to his daughter, and which put out the unintended message that there was something negative about being different.

In each of these true stories, someone close to the adoptee tried to neutralize or scramble their ethnic identity. For some people, "different" implies "threatening." Thus the once-popular melting pot idea implied that individual racial or cultural identities should be absorbed into the dominant ones through assimilation. This idea can be precarious for transracially adopted children, especially teens, who have a natural and overriding desire to fit in with peers as well as family members. So if you were raised in an atmosphere of color blindness together with the usual pressure to assimilate, your racial and cultural identities might have become muffled.

"I don't see my son's color. Race is just not an issue for us."

When family or friends proclaim that they do not notice your color, they don't completely see you. And if this occurred in your childhood, it probably made it harder for you to forge your identity, or to prepare yourself for challenges out there beyond your front door.

We don't have to assume that every person who embraces colorblindness is consciously racist; surely some are not. Those who claim to be race-neutral in their outlook may be coming from a sincere desire to make you feel included. Or they may be expressing their longing for a raceless world, a "utopia" which they imagine would obliterate racism altogether. Maybe they believe that race-based prejudice is a thing of the past, and are completely unaware that they are speaking from inside a white bubble. It is also likely that they have no idea that, words like "I don't see you as Asian/ Black/Latino" are *not* affirming. They are negating.

Whatever the motivations, seeing you-minus-your-racial and ethnic identity is an effort to erase an essential part of who you obviously are. This attitude also ignores what may be the clearest, most accessible link to your history: The face that looks back at you from the mirror.

～

"One thing that has really bothered me getting older is how I was just assumed to assimilate into their culture and not have any of mine. I grew up knowing nothing about my birth place, my birth culture, real heritage… And I didn't know about these things (like culture camps) as a kid. I mean, like that hurts too. Were you like actively shielding me away from that stuff? I mean, bless their hearts, they're great people and they're always going to be my parents. But they totally have the 'we-don't-see-color' mindset. It's really, as I've gotten older, really upsetting and disappointing.

*"It's a huge irony. I know they (my parents) were coming from love, from a good place, but, honestly, they set me up for even worse failure. Like how I felt about myself. And also, at the end of the day, it's kind of disrespectful, invalidating as a human being. Where you came from is not worthy…or is not at least equal. I mean, that's absurd to me. It's an upsetting aspect, absolutely." —*DEVON

～

"I have a great relationship with my parents. They were amazing parents in a lot of ways. But the whole narrative of our family was, 'We don't see color, we're all equal, we're all the same.' But that didn't help me, especially when I hit puberty and started to notice people started to treat me differently.

"It was basically like, 'Race is Shannon's problem,' instead of,

'When we adopted you, a black child, we became an interracial family.'" —SHANNON GIBNEY[26]

∼

"But, let's be real, of course, you see that I'm Asian. It's the first thing you notice, whether you're aware of it or not. I mean, look at my hair and eyes and skin—of course, you and every other White person see that I'm Asian. Other Asian people see that I'm Asian.

"And if you really want to mean it when you say to me, 'I just see you as you', then you would recognize that being Asian is an inextricable, undeniable part of who I am. I ain't ashamed of it... and neither should you be. But just don't use the recognition of my race to treat me with disrespect—that's where you start to go wrong...

"...Being non-racist does not mean pretending that you do not see the color of someone's skin or hear the way that they speak or smell the food that they eat. Being non-racist means you see all these things without devaluing them, or thinking they're somehow less than your Whiteness." —MILA KONOMOS[27]

∼

We can and must allow each person's uniqueness to have equal value. We do not have to travel the counterfeit path to self-esteem by placing ourselves above one another. It's much more effective to cultivate a positive sense of who we are, within ourselves—and to strongly support each other to do the same. The colorblind or melting pot approach (like microaggressions, but more on that later) are undermining forces. Although one might seem gentler than the other, over time both potentially have the impact of corroding self-esteem.

While some people still strive for sameness, we Americans are in fact more diverse than ever and our population will continue to evolve in that direction. By 2045, whites will no longer be in the majority. According to U.S. Census statistics, racial minorities altogether will be the major demographic growth group going forward. And within our vividly pluralistic society of the future, the fastest growing group will be those of mixed race.[28]

The melting pot idea has not obliterated our racial and cultural differences, or the negative ways in which we may deal with them. Families who seek out diverse schools and neighborhoods for their internationally adopted kids and cultivate a multi-cultural family identity give them a major advantage: A more user-friendly launching pad to the outside world. Because inevitably, kids do step outside their front doors and need to navigate the terrain of school and community—not to mention the wider world of media and society.

THERE IS RACE
AND THERE IS CULTURE

In many adoptive families, exploring culture just seems like an easier, more fun pursuit than wading into issues of race. Learning how to make chapatis or empanadas, celebrating Moon Festival or joining other adoptive families at culture camp are all meaningful activities which validate a child's heritage. But while the culture camp experience might well be wonderful and empowering, a single week-long session in the summertime cannot provide total cultural immersion. Nor will any of these fun-filled experiences substitute for taking on issues of race and racism—or actively cultivating a positive identity as a multi-racial family, ideally in a diverse community.

Here are reactions of several adoptees:

"My parents tried to raise us in a colorblind sort of utopia and we weren't prepared for the negativity that we were going to get

about our (African-American) brother. We didn't understand it, and we didn't know how to handle it...We thought that everybody loved everyone, and color didn't matter...until middle school." —CARMEN[29]

~

"My parents never once tried to play down any of my concerns about race." Journalist Collier Myerson describes this experience of an Indian adoptee whose parents never tried to play down his concerns about race. In fact, they were proactive in teaching him and his two siblings (also adopted from India) about their birth country with books and news stories. The family attended culture camps and were members of a group of families who had adopted children from India. All of this proved helpful. But in sixth grade, issues of racial difference pushed to the surface. And by the time he reached high school, he realized that race was a larger issue than he had previously thought. [30]

~

"Adoptees should have 'lived' experiences related to adoption and race: Traveling to birth countries, attending racially diverse schools. Those things might have helped, but only along with parents who were willing to be honest about racism." —LAURA KLUNDER[31]

OVERZEALOUS AND UNDERZEALOUS PARENTS—WHERE'S THE BALANCE?

"I was really lucky that when I needed that cultural connection, my mom would provide it. But even when I didn't want it, she continued to provide it, when I just wanted to be a normal white kid at that moment. It was hard to express at the time. I felt a little pressure from my mom to be Indian." —MALLORY

∼

"My mother said to me, 'But you didn't grow up Vietnamese' (when I expressed interest in visiting Vietnam, learning more about my heritage). But from my point of view, I did in ways that she didn't understand...Everything is magnetized in a small town. Every room I've ever walked into, I've been a minority... feeling that you're a gimmick or a sidekick makes you become a clown or a trouble-maker...As an Asian male (in a small town) it's hard to find girls to have a relationship with...You're considered undesirable...I asked this girl to dance in high school and she said no. And that stuck with me my entire dating life. It wasn't until I was aware of the stereotypes that I felt that I was Asian." —DAVID

∼

"My parents were adamant about connecting me with Chinese culture—possibly because I was adopted at age five. I went to China every summer. I tried to be 'normal' by not talking about adoption." —JENNI FANG LEE [32]

∼

And these comments from two internationally adopted teens participating in a group discussion:

∼

"You don't want them to forget their culture, but you don't want to, like, obsess over it. Then you're making it obvious that you don't belong here." —ANONYMOUS

"We are not 'just Americans' like our parents and others in our communities." —ANONYMOUS

Some parents may feel it's best to wait for their son or daughter to express a desire to learn about their birth culture, to talk about race, or to meet other adoptees because they want these experiences to be child-led rather than imposed. One interviewee described her childhood experience this way:

"I attended a picnic once for families with Chinese adoptees and thought it was odd—I felt out of place...My parents always told me that if I wanted to know something about my culture they would help...but I was never introduced to the idea of culture camps...my parents were waiting for me to initiate interest and I never did... I do not feel a strong connection to Chinese culture...But I would love to go back to the town I came from and the orphanage. I have photos of the orphanage...and a blanket from China that my dad brought when he came to get me that I still sleep with."—ALLISON

∿

It is possible that parents like Allison's might worry that introducing the subject of cultural or racial difference would make her feel she didn't quite belong to the family, that she was somehow different—and why risk weakening those family bonds? Adoptees might feel hesitant to express their interest in racial issues or birth culture for a host of reasons. But silence may not be so golden in this situation. It's likely that adoptees already feel different and need to have that acknowledged in a healthy and loving way.

The light touch in connection with the subjects of culture and race might also feel invalidating. Minimizing the importance of these issues can actually weaken family bonds, chilling communication and trust, while piling on self-doubt, and even shame—an impact most parents would certainly not intend, but...

∿

"I never went to camp, I never went to classes. A few years ago, when I was starting to get involved in Korean stuff I must have made a comment to my parents about not having done that stuff, and my mom said, 'Well, you never showed an interest.' And I thought 'I

never showed an interest in school either and that didn't prevent you from sending me.'" —From an interview by KIM JA PARK NELSON[33]

TALK IS NOT CHEAP

If you happen to be a human being, you have your biases. We all have them; it's that simple. The trick is for each of us to understand what those biases are, and where they come from. That ongoing awareness then becomes the springboard for meaningful exchange between people.

Now back to family, friends, coworkers and nearly everyone else: Why is the discussion of racial and cultural differences often such a taboo topic? Maybe some people just lack awareness, or don't have the language to enter into such conversations, or have a fear, perhaps unnamed. What exactly is the hurdle—knowledge, words, courage? Or all three?

If you're an adoptee of color, you might think that expressing race-related thoughts, experiences, or questions would underline misunderstanding and isolation in your family or community, making things worse instead of better. Perhaps it would be too emotional, unleashing defensiveness and blame. Or maybe it would rip off the veil of harmony, leaving you feeling shocked and wounded.

The problem is that *not* talking about racism doesn't make it go away.

∾

"So it's my family, too, whenever I would try to bring up racial issues, it was stopped. And if I talked about it, for instance, in an email that I wrote my sister...she wrote back, saying 'It must be really hard, but we saved you and, you know, you should be, in a way, grateful that we did this' and all this stuff. So, I can't really talk to my family about it. They really don't understand, they think that I

should just be able to get over it." —From an interview by KIM JA PARK NELSON[34]

A simple truth: People in the majority have a hard time fully appreciating what it's like to be in the minority. As one white teacher said to me when we were discussing issues of unintended exclusion of minority children at the school: "Being in the majority gives us amnesia."

Whether amnesiac or not, members of the dominant racial group may often feel hesitant, or downright lost, when it comes to discussing matters of race or cultural difference for fear of stumbling wrongly or hurtfully into such a conversation. They might also worry that acknowledging racial differences is itself racist, and they disown that label. They also might, as in my situation as a parent, have unrealistic (whitewashed) expectations about how much racism their child might encounter in the community.

The assumption of white privilege, conscious or not, brings with it expectations of entitlement, status, and open opportunities. It might include beliefs like "white=normal" and "American= white." For those not fully aware of their bias, it can distort ideas about behavior, beauty, and achievement—and blind them to the everyday suffering of people of color.

Again, Laura Klunder:

"You need parents who can talk about white privilege, who can say 'You might experience some of this. I'm sorry. We are in this together.'" [35]

In other words, awareness, curiosity and empathy create the ground for conversation about any sensitive subject, including race. And that conversation can be powerfully helpful just as its absence can be harmful.

"I am 18. I'm the oldest of 8 children. And when I was 13, two of my siblings were adopted from Guatemala. So they were both Latino

and the rest of my family is Caucasian...We keep a really open dialogue about race in our house. You know, we talk about it. We're very conscious of it, but we're still navigating it...The most important thing I want to say about this topic is, you know, while we address race in our home and while we're conscious of it, it is nowhere near the most important part of our family."[36]

~

"I no longer think of adoption in terms of good or bad, but realistic and unrealistic. I would explain that my own parents tried very hard to be good parents, and in many ways were good parents, and we did not have a single honest conversation about race until I was in my late twenties and are still dealing with the consequences of that." —Nicole Soojung Callahan [37]

~

Here is another comment about transracial adoptees finding their identities, from an anonymous source:

"It's hard to be the only non-white face in your neighborhood or class of white kids. It's not even that people are racist—though for sure this is true sometimes. It's that it's important to see your own face reflected back at you once in awhile—and not just when you stand in front of a mirror. It's important to know that your roots—where you came from—are worthy and valid. That your racial identity is important, even if it's not the most important thing...And sometimes, you know, it's cool to be around folks who get you in a different way than your parents. Sometimes you need that, and sometimes it just feels right...Connecting with your birth family...doesn't always work out, and then we have to find role models and mentors who can help us connect with our racial heritage. It's part of who we are and it's important. No one should say it isn't."

~

It's not only parents who may be reluctant to bring up discussions of this sensitive subject: Adoptees sometimes hesitate as well.

*"I was going to talk with my parents last weekend about this stuff, but we were having a really nice time and I didn't want to ruin it." —*DEVON

It *is* possible that such a discussion would backfire. You might even regret it—especially if you expect complete and total understanding in return for expressing yourself. But short of that, achieving more visibility and empathy for you as a person together with your own sense of being more authentic with those closest to you could make the effort worthwhile.

These conversations don't have to happen cold. You can prepare by talking with trusted adoptee friends or doing some relevant reading, such as *We Can All Get Along: 50 Steps You Can Take to Help End Racism at Home, at Work, in Your Community* by Clyde W. Ford, or Ijeoma Oluo's *So You Want to Talk About Race.* These are two very different sources that can help stimulate your thinking not only about the importance of having conversations about race but how you might go about initiating or participating in them. Delve into these books or other resources you discover and see which points resonate for you.

However, if after all the prep and thought you put into it, you still feel hesitant, ask yourself *why*. There may be valid reasons. Fear of broaching the subject of race is not necessarily baseless or crazy. First and foremost, you need to assess the safety of the environment. Are these people strangers or friends or family and how does that affect you? Is anyone being verbally abusive or is their attitude open and respectful? Are there allies in the group or are you outnumbered? What does your gut tell you about the situation?

The main point here is that if the appropriate opportunity exists for dialogue that might foster more understanding, you have the possibility to be seen more fully for who you are. And to be strengthened by your own courage.

And one more thing: Knowing and being who you are without apology might make others uncomfortable at times, but it is not your job to submerge yourself in the interest of their comfort. And—paying it forward—when you educate others and encourage them to be fully who *they* are, *everyone* rises.

MICROAGGRESSIONS: RACISM'S STEALTHY SIBLING

Do any of the following comments or questions sound familiar?

"So...what ARE you?"

"You look so different from your family pictures."

"Your family looks weird."

"Your skin looks so dirty. Did you fall in the mud or something?"

"Twinkie/Banana/Oreo."

"Where are you REALLY from? You don't have an accent."

"How much did your parents pay for you?"

"What do you eat on Thanksgiving?"

"You're really pretty for a dark girl."

"Why do you sound so white?"

"Can you see as much as white people do? Because of your eyes, I mean."

"Ya'know, you don't act like a normal black (or Asian or Latino) person. You're different."

"We don't see you as Asian/Black/Latino. We just see you as you."

"I'm so glad you people are here. I mean, not everybody is, but I am."

The list above is a collection of real life comments, and did not spring from my imagination.

Racism appears in many guises, from casual to blatant, unconscious to deliberate. Stereotyping minority groups, asserting that white is the standard for normal, minimizing discrimination or the pain of racism, and expressing discomfort with a particular racial group all have the effect, intended or not, of isolating and inflicting hurt.

Blatant racism is unmistakable: Name-calling. Race-based exclusion and bullying. Racial violence. Horrifying elements of our world that unfortunately many transnational adoptees have experienced, often by grade school, in the classroom, on the playground, or on the school bus. Sometimes even within their own families.

In their subtler form, casual racism and microaggressions can be confusing whether you're on the receiving end or witnessing the remarks as they find their target. You might not even recognize them for the kind of comment they actually are—somehow you just feel bad without knowing exactly why.

～

"A girl at school said, 'Why don't you just go back to Vietnam?' After being confronted by the teacher about her remark, she said, 'Oh, I just meant it would be nice for her to travel to Vietnam. She's just too sensitive.' So my mom called her mom and she said, 'Oh, no, she couldn't have said that. Her best friend is African-American.'" —LINH

Because microaggressions may be pint-sized, common, and even subtle, some people ask, *"What's the big deal?"*

The big deal is that these messages soak in over time—an acid drip that corrodes your good feelings about yourself. Or, more starkly, in the words of Ojibway Shaman/Elder, Dr. Duke Redbird, enduring microaggressions is like "death by 1,000 cuts." [38]

When someone looks at you and stretches out their eyelids, the message is *you don't belong.* Or when you were young, and a cashier glanced at you then commented to your mom, "They sure are making them dark these days, aren't they?" the message was that somehow *your skin color was a defect.* If a store owner singles you out to follow around their shop because your skin is brown, he or she is expressing a microaggression without even saying a word.

Communications like these can have a snowball effect over time, making you feel isolated and unsafe for simply being who you are. Studies have shown that over time microaggressions can cause anxiety, high blood pressure, and depression, in part because they are under the radar, tough to spot, and hard to respond to. [39]

Pay attention to your body signals. When you hear such a remark, does your stomach tighten? Do you clench your teeth? Does your breathing become shallow? It's important to learn to read between the lines of statements that cause you to feel uncomfortable.

Below is a vivid example of microaggressions and their impact:

"I was sitting in Driver's Ed in a classroom full of high schoolers and one girl was particularly nervous about passing her driving test. She kept expressing her concerns and talking about how anxious she was, and the guy sitting next to her—a white boy dressed in Vans and a white 'Diamond Mining Co.' t-shirt—stated flatly 'At least you're not Asian, 'cause then you'd fail for sure.'

"A tight-feeling of anger immediately took over my entire body

and tears started to form behind my eyes; I managed to blink them away and replace them with a scowl that settled on my face. I felt embarrassed, angry, and resentful that he could act so carelessly like that; those words fell out of his mouth without missing a beat. He probably didn't even realize that I had overheard what he was saying. Or maybe he didn't even see me at all. That's probably what hurt the most.

"There are definitely times when people make these remarks with the intention of causing pain and don't care that someone else is getting hurt in the process. But there are also times when I wonder if people even realize that there are actual human beings on the receiving end of these jokes. I want people who make these racist comments and who think their jokes are funny to understand that their words are powerful; they have meaning, and they can cause a great deal of pain."—JAEUN PARK[40]

"FRIENDLY" HUMOR AND "COMPLIMENTS"

"With my college friends…my ethnicity was discussed only within the framework of comedy, as if being the only person of color in a group of white people was always hilarious. I thought this humor helped me own my ethnicity, but it only created more distance between my identity and my ethnicity. Throughout my young adult life, I carried around this sense of being lonely, even in a crowd of people."
—SHELISE GIESEKE[41]

⁓

Being the only person of color in a group of white people is …funny?? The banter may appear friendly and light-hearted, but the message is not. A joke or a compliment is not always what it seems. Fancy wrapping decorated with nice words does not always contain a gift.

What about those so-called positive stereotypes? "Model minority." "Math genius." "Super athlete." "You people are always *so* chill." "You're really pretty for a black girl." "Your English is sooo good!"

When you flip over these "compliments," you find they are often linked to negative messages. If someone assumes you are a math genius because you are Asian, the underside of this seemingly nice statement might be an assumption about your physical weakness. If you are a black college student and a white student asks which sport you play, are they simply complimenting you for your strength or grace? Or are they also implying that you must have been admitted on the basis of athletics alone, rather than for your academic ability? If someone praises you as an attractive *exception* to your racial or ethnic group, they are insulting the other members of the group. And if a person expresses amazement about your excellent English, they are labeling you as a foreigner solely because of your physical features, someone who couldn't *truly* belong.

By the way, if you do have a particular talent that is *outside* someone's stereotype of your group, should you be told that you're a credit to your race? Why not simply be given that credit for excelling on your own? It would certainly be unusual for a white person to ever receive that kind of feedback for a job well done, feedback linking achievement to whiteness instead of giving them credit as an individual.

Whether uttered in positive or negative language, microaggressions can spring from complete ignorance or utter insensitivity. "Hey, what do they speak in your country? Asian?" A Korean-born grad student recounts how one of her professors kept confusing her with a student from Latin America. The two women looked absolutely nothing alike—except that they were both women of color.

Ignorant comments still sting, even if they are not deliberately negative. But it's important not to conflate intention and behavior. Ignorance or innocence do not erase words that have already met their target. Language has power. Once delivered, it makes an impact. Now what do you do?

RESPONDING

One six-year-old Vietnamese adoptee was problem-solving with her mother about how to respond to hateful remarks by classmates. The child offered this idea: "I would just say to them, 'It's not okay to make fun of people. Someday *you* may be Vietnamese, too.'"

While the innocence of this remark might make you smile as it did me, the important thing here is that even in her young way of perceiving, this child was beginning to climb out of victim mode and to craft a plan of action.

There is no shortage of opportunities for educating people, and fortifying ourselves in the process. When you hear a racial or ethnic slur (or a negative comment about adoption, for that matter)—even if it isn't aimed at you personally—will you speak up? By remaining quiet, you are signaling that such statements are acceptable, that it is okay to put down those who are perceived as different. You might ask yourself, how did you respond to microaggressions or racist comments in the past? And what could you do differently when that next situation presents itself? Because it will.

But first and always, determine if you are in a safe environment. Are there any physical threats lurking? Are you outnumbered? What is your gut telling you?

Assuming you determine that the red lights aren't flashing and it's safe to launch a conversation, which kind of response would most accurately reflect your feelings and values? Are you able to respond calmly in the moment? Can you think of how you might inspire others to change their behavior by modeling the type of communication you would appreciate—minus the sarcasm and putdowns? Explain the full impact of their words. You can imagine that you will have a better chance of being heard if you can limit your comments to those which focus on the specific, hurtful behavior rather than demonizing the person involved.

Of course, there are no guarantees how those on the receiving end will react, no matter how carefully you craft your language. They might be receptive. "I'm really glad you brought this up. I had no idea." Or defensive: "You misinterpreted me. Don't be so sensitive. I didn't mean it that way." So be it. You can listen, and then offer your explanation about why the remark offended you. And you can certainly move on (and probably should) if the conversation seems unproductive. The goal is to communicate, not to score a victory.

It can also be useful to ask questions. If someone asks "Where are you from? I mean where are you *really* from?" you could say simply, "I was born in Peru and I grew up in Baltimore. I'm wondering why you asked me that question. What do you mean?" And then be open to hearing input, listening carefully to what's being said, perhaps even repeating it back to make sure you got it right. Asking questions and listening attentively can definitely enhance the exchange.

Cultivating allies is important, too. Assemble your kindred spirits and create a plan to stand up to microaggressions together— in the classroom, around the dinner table, on the bus, at a party.

In the end, given that the environment is a safe one, making a few people uncomfortable with frank talk about race, cultural difference (or adoption) is a small price to pay for the conversation itself.

• • •

Think back: What kind of preparation did you get during childhood for dealing with racism? Growing up, you may or may not have had the modeling you needed to deal with these situations.

Indeed, white parents do not always grasp what the experiences of their adopted children of color feel like. Some might not even be comfortable knowing. They might also equate microaggressions with the commonplace rude and annoying behavior they themselves often deal with in daily life. But, of course, it is *not* the same.

Looking back on her childhood, Jesse recalled that her parents suggested that she respond to racist remarks with humor. However, she felt this advice did not help her learn how to be effective in those situations and, in this way, she felt unsupported. As warm and positive as her relationship with her parents was, it lacked an understanding or expressed interest in what it was like for Jesse to be on the receiving end of racist comments.

Another adoptee remembered a summer camp experience when another camper taunted her with "I hate the color brown. I don't want to play with you." Her counselor's advice was to just ignore the offenses, but the adoptive mother reported the incident to the director, suggesting ideas and materials to improve counselor training specifically around issues of racial bullying. Even though the adoptee herself never wished to return to that camp, she did feel supported by her mother's efforts and it helped her learn to self-advocate. In this situation, the camp director did follow the suggestions about the additional counselor training to deal with these problems.

Another adoptee who appreciated his parent's response to racial bullying:

"I was like in fifth grade and I was riding the school bus...and some of the junior and senior kids were just incessant...on and on with their racial slurs, and they were pretty nasty about it. And then one day after a couple of weeks my (White) brother got up and just said, 'Hey, just shut up. Knock it off!' And so they hit him on the head with a book...My mom used to always wait for us, as we got

off the bus, and saw this big 'ole red welt on (my brother's) head. And so the very next day, the boys and their mothers and fathers were in our living room…You know, I think the guys were actually nicer to me because they felt bad for what they did, rather than just because they had to." — From interview by KIM JA PARK NELSON [42]

⌒

Adoptee Laura Klunder did not believe that her parents recognized racism.

"I knew that I was the only person of color in their life, and it was too easy for them to invalidate my point of view as another 'anger issue'."—LAURA KLUNDER [43]

⌒

One teen offers this advice to adoptive parents: *"Don't say 'I'm sure he didn't mean it.' Don't try to fix it. Say, 'That stinks!'"*

THE WAY FORWARD

Recognizing and countering bigotry, both outside and within ourselves, is an important piece of finding and embracing identity if you are a transracial adoptee. And this is, in fact, an ongoing challenge which calls to each of us regardless of our skin color.

Having a learning mode/action mode attitude will keep you engaged in the process. In fact, sometimes the most meaningful learning comes from giving what you offer others. Some examples: Sharing what you've gained from your own journey through writing articles or joining adoptee groups online, working within organizations that support international adoptees or being a counselor at a culture camp. There are many ways to reach out—and helping others make sense of things and tap into their own wisdom also helps you process what you have learned over time.

⌒

"Going to Heritage Camp as an adult performer was a really power-ful experience for me because I had never really been around other adoptees before. There were kids who are going through identity issues that I had been through when I was younger and I was able to share my experiences with them. It was a very powerful experience for me...I wonder how important that would have been to me when I was younger, but I never had it." —NIKO

CONNECT, CONNECT, CONNECT

One thing many international adoptees have found deeply helpful is reaching out to other transcountry adoptees. Claim the connections that make most sense to you. Gather together whatever pieces of your history are available. Explore your birth culture, keeping in mind that this is a work in progress—complicated, at times frustrating or even painful. At other moments immensely satisfying. Your identity is waiting to take shape.

This is a quest you *don't* have to undertake alone. When things are rough, and you feel ungrounded, you don't have to simply endure. Isolation stokes bad feelings. Establishing meaningful connections, reading about the experiences of other transracial adoptees, and finding your own affinity groups can make all the difference in the world. Shared experience, shared pride—even shared doubts—can validate your feelings, clarify perceptions, raise your self-esteem, and remind you of your courage.

After all, as an international adoptee you are, by definition, a survivor and a person of resilience.

The community of intercountry adoptees has expanded expo-nentially in the past two decades, online and otherwise. You can read, listen, or chat with those who express thought-provoking insights, compassion, anger, and everything else you can imagine that relates to your own experience. Some of the input will be helpful. Some will not really speak to you. Put your feelers out and then be a good filter for yourself. Or find a trusted person who can lend their experience and their judgement.

While some may still be pining for a society populated by people of the same race and culture, the world as we know it *is* colorful and splendidly multi-cultural—and becoming more so all the time. Finding your place in this landscape can be challenging, especially for those who were born in other countries and look different from their adoptive families.

~

"I grew up in rural Minnesota...decent size small town of 13,000. But it was isolating, alienating where I was made to feel a lot different growing up. I literally stuck out in lots of situations. Growing up I could count all the people of color in my school on two hands in grades above and below me...From age four to nine, I was a pretty sad kid. I was pretty introverted. I bottled a lot of things up. I used to cry myself to sleep at night. It was tough to deal with at times. I thought about it a lot, the town, how people were, that part of the country...How wildly insensitive it is to throw this little baby into Wonder Bread America...There was no question that I had to get out as fast as I could.

"...Aside from the race stuff, the mental health stuff should have been addressed my whole life. And being a man, I was taught to pull yourself up by your bootstraps...almost ashamed of feelings. Like it was weak to ask for help. Maybe it's partly just being an American, too.

"Yeah, it is hard to keep stuff in. That was a big part of joining adoptee groups. Hugely therapeutic, a big reason why people are in those groups. I've grown up around adoptees all my life, but I honestly had no idea there were other people out there exactly like me talking about everything I had felt my entire life. So that was

132

very empowering and just very helpful. We can thank the internet for that one." —DEVON

~

"I went to a completely white elementary school. By the end of elementary school, I completely hated it and chose to go to a school with a majority black population. It was definitely better. Kids called me 'blackie.' I went pretty ghetto and wore corn rows in my hair every day...I thought I was black. But once I joined my Indian dance group, I became really Indian and proud to be Indian. I think a lot of it [the transition] was learning a lot about my culture and learning what it is to be Indian. I was very aware of how cool my culture was. There was a group of us adoptees within the dance group and we all became very close." —MALLORY

~

The current political climate in the U.S., with its strong anti-immigrant and overtly racist overtones, can make any person of color feel more visible and vulnerable than ever before. This makes it all the more important to find kindred spirits to connect with so your experiences and questions can emerge in safe space. Many things that may seem weird when you are alone with them often feel acceptable and more normal when shared.

~

"I continued this self-deprecation until I went to college and took an Introduction to Asian American Studies course, where I learned about the harmful effects of racism and what it meant to be an Asian-American person. For the first time in my life, I was in an environment where I was not the only person who experienced race-related discrimination. However, since I didn't have anyone to relate with before this moment, it was an overwhelming, yet comforting experience to realize that I was in fact not alone...I realized I

wasn't able to genuinely belong until I no longer had to try to belong. Rather, I belonged the most when I was surrounded by people who understood my experiences on an implicit and personal level, where I could be my true self *and didn't have to fit in anymore. 'Coming out' as Asian-American...was one of the most profound moments of self-discovery for me..."*—ERICA GEHRINGER[44]

⁓

"Family members wouldn't say anything directly racist to me. But growing up... people would say things they didn't think were racist, but I did definitely think it was subtle racism, things that would make me feel a little bit more different. It kind of pushed me to find Asian groups that I could relate to where I could feel I fit in." —NIKO

⁓

We all need our people—whatever that lights up for us: Fellow adoptees, those with similar racial or ethnic backgrounds, or a broad diversity that presents multiple opportunities for belonging. And sometimes switching up your environment is a priority, a choice you might well have as an adult that you might not have had as a child.

⁓

"Kids need to be in diversified communities so they can see people who look like them—so they don't freak out. I was blessed to have been raised in Prince George's County with so many inspirational black people." —ASELEFECH EVANS [45]

⁓

"My brother and I were some of the few minorities in a small school district. We felt much better when we moved to a larger school district with racial and socioeconomic diversity. I also suggest traveling to diverse cities. Seeing other people who look like you helps a lot when

you're growing up and figuring out how you belong and perhaps where you belong."—MEGGAN ELLINGBOE[46]

As a parent, I remember the experience of moving to a large city and watching so many positive feelings unfold for our daughter: Self-acceptance, pride and a sense of belonging. She was finally in the midst of a city alive with diversity and was illuminated by it.

HOMELAND TRAVEL: THE POWER OF BEING THERE

Homeland travel can be tantalizing and terrifying.

Many options are available if you have the desire and opportunity to make the journey. Tour groups with or without your adoptive family, service trips or solo journeys—including birth parent searches or not. Regardless of which option you choose, each is imbedded with a gamut of emotions, from curiosity, wonder and joy to grief, and back again

Homeland visits raise some questions while answering others. Some wounds may open while others may begin to heal. For example, if you are a transracial adoptee returning to your birth country, the idea that human beauty exists in myriad forms and colors, becomes an obvious and overwhelming truth.

These trips can provide a powerful opportunity to tap into feelings you may experience while you have support in the wings. They can also bring personal history into present life—while also potentially awakening a sense of longing for connection that seems just out of reach due to language and cultural barriers, a common frustration. Yet despite the inherent complications, homeland travel can often animate a more complete sense of who you are as you see where you first entered the world.

∾

"When I visited China, I thought about what my life would have been like if I had grown up in the orphanage like this one boy did who my mom recognized. It was comforting to visit and see how it really was. I definitely want to go back someday."

∽

"My parents never said they were proud of me nor did they reach out to me to find out what I was experiencing. They had great interest in Latin American cultures, but not in mine. So I got the message that it was ok to be different on the one hand, but, on the other hand, my cultures (African-American and Vietnamese) were invisible. Although they did retain my Vietnamese name, I grew up hating it. I didn't get the validation I needed.

"But then, when I was in my mid-20's, I found out that my parents had been saving money for years for this purpose (visiting my birth country). This was so powerful for me, all the love and validation that I had longed for all these years. They went to Vietnam with me. I brought along the photo of the nun who had taken care of me in the orphanage and I was able to find her. She remembered me. Ten years later, I still haven't gotten over this meeting."—KENNY

∽

The following quotes are from adoptees of various ages regarding their experiences with group heritage journeys with the Ties Adoptive Family Travel program,[47] one of a number that facilitate homeland journeys for adoptees:

∽

"Whenever anyone asked questions about the circumstances of my birth and adoption or my birth country, I recited it like I was telling a story about someone else. When I got to my birth country, all of that changed."

∽

"It turned my grey (adoptive experience) impressions into Technicolor."

~

"I learned who I truly am. I knew I was adopted from China, born in Anhui Province, found somewhere in Tongling City, but when you actually get a chance to go back to your roots, everything seems to come together."

~

"Before I traveled, I wondered what could have been so bad in my birth country that my birth parents couldn't or wouldn't raise me. I saw pictures, even a movie, but it seemed like no one could be that poor, like maybe it was an old movie or an old picture from a long time ago. Not now."

~

Aside from travelling to the place of your birth, you can actively seek and create a healthy environment for yourself here in your adopted country. Draw strength and support from friends, mentors, family or through materials you read. As much as possible surround yourself with those who reflect and respect your unique identity. Take advantage of the resources that abound, from books and articles to affinity groups, blogs, and websites, YouTube channels and travel opportunities. Check the Resource page for ideas.

Listen. Read. Write. Speak what is true for *you.* Language is powerful, including your own. Journal, write poetry and songs. Dance, sculpt, paint, photograph. Check out exhibits and performances of other adoptee artists. Engage in conversation and gain perspective.

It is for you to claim this quest as your own—as you tackle college, enter the workforce, travel the world, or become parents yourselves—regardless of your starting point and how amazing, flawed, or less than perfect your childhood was.

This is Your History. Your Lineage. Your Culture(s). Your Color(s). Complex and uniquely interesting.

PICK UP YOUR PEN

1. How do you define racism?

_____

_____

_____

_____

_____

2. What are your triggers when witnessing or discussing stereotyping, discrimination or racism?

_____

_____

_____

_____

_____

3. What are your stereotypes of different groups, including your own? Where do you think they came from?

_____

_____

_____

_____

_____

4. One Asian American says that not a day passes in which she does not experience her race in a negative way, either in person or through the media. Does that statement resonate for you?

_____

_____

_____

_____

_____

5. How did your parents, siblings, teachers, and friends deal with microaggressions? What was positive, supportive or educational in their responses? Would you have handled it differently, and if so how?

_____

_____

_____

_____

_____

6. How have you yourself been confronted with such incidents in the past? What seems to have worked best for you in handling them?

_____

_____

_____

_____

_____

7. Most of us evolve as we grow older and refine our responses. What have you learned over time?

_____

_____

_____

_____

8. What would you like to do to strengthen your racial, ethnic or cultural identity?

_____

_____

_____

_____

_____

End Notes

14 "My Skin Is Not Me" excerpt, To Be Me, Teen Ink, *Huffington Post,* September 9, 2009.

15 "Amid decline in international adoptions to US..." by Abby Budiman and Mark Hugo Lopez, FACTANK, Pew Research Center, October 17, 2017.

16 U.S. Department of Health and Human Services, "Adoption USA, A Chartbook Based on the 2007 Survey of Adoptive Parents. Race, Ethnicity and Gender," November 1, 2009.

17 "Race Is a Social Construct, Scientists Argue," Megan Gannon, Live Science, *Scientific American,* February 5, 2016.

18 Amy Lee Scott, Land of Gazillion Adoptees interview, October 16, 2012.

19 Mila C. Konomos, "Yoon's Blur blog," April 9, 2013.

20 "Beyond Culture Camp: Promoting Positive Identity Formation in Adoption," Evan B. Donaldson Adoption Institute study, November 9, 2009.

21 "Did You Ever Mind It? Thoughts on Race and Adoption" by Nicole Soojung Callahan, November 11, 2014.

22 Mila Konomos,"Yoon's Blur Blog," date unknown.

23 "Twice Foreign" by Shelise Gieseke, *Adoption Mosaic Magazine,* approx. 2011.

24 "Outside the Margins" by Erica Gehringer, *Gazillion Voices Magazine,* date unknown.

25 Amy Lee Scott, LGA interview, October 16, 2012.

26 Shannon Gibney, *MPR News,* "Magazine for adult adoptees raises issues of alienation, racism and loss" by Laura Yuen, August 5, 2013.

27 Mila Konomos, "Yoon's Blur Blog," date unknown.

28 "The US will become 'minority white' in 2045, Census projects" by William H. Frey, Brookings "The Avenue," updated September 10, 2018.

29 "The Parenting Dilemmas of Transracial Adoption" NPR Talk of the Nation, May 11, 2011.

30 "What Happens When Transnational Adoptees Learn About Race?" by Collier Myerson, Talking Points Memo, The Slice, January 30, 2015.

31 "Why a Generation of Adoptees Is Returning to South Korea" by Maggie Jones, *New York Times Magazine,* January 14, 2015.

32 Aselefech Evans and Jenni Fang Lee conversation, YouTube, December 3, 2013 https://youtu.be/NDC3N1S1601

33 "Korean Looks, American Eyes: Korean American Adoptees, Race, Culture and Nation" by Kim Ja Park Nelson, University of Minnesota, Department of American Studies, December, 2009.

34 "Korean Looks, American Eyes: Korean American Adoptees, Race, Culture and Nation" by Kim Ja Park Nelson, University of Minnesota, Department of American Studies, December, 2009.

35 "Why a Generation of Adoptees Is Returning to South Korea" by Maggie Jones, *New York Times Magazine*, January 14, 2015.

36 "The Parenting Dilemmas of Transracial Adoption," NPR Talk of the Nation, May 11, 2011.

37 "Did You Ever Mind It? Thoughts on Race and Adoption" by Nicole Soojung Callahan, The Toast, November 11, 2014.

38 "Racist Microaggressions Are Like Death By A Thousand Cuts" by Jeewan Chanicka, Huffpost, March 19, 2018.

39 "How Racism and Microaggressions Lead to Worse Health" by Gina Torino,   USC Center for Health Journalism, November 10, 2017.

40 "The Pain of Casual Racism" by Jaeun Park, *BuzzFeed News*, November 16, 2014.

41 "Twice Foreign" by Shelise Gieseke, *Adoption Mosaic Magazine*, approx. 2011.

42 "Korean Looks, American Eyes" by Kim Ja Park Nelson, University of Minnesota, Department of American Studies, December, 2009.

43 "Why a Generation of Adoptees is Returning to South Korea" by Maggie Jones, *New York Times Magazine*, January 14, 2015.

44 "Outside the Margins" by Erica Gehringer, Gazillion Voices Magazine, date unknown.

45 Aselefech Evans and Jenni Fang Lee conversation, YouTube, December 3, 2013 https://youtube/NDC3N1S1601.

46 "What are your experiences as an adoptee?" Meggan Ellingboe, Minnesota Public Radio Daily Circuit Blog, July 10, 2012.

47 "Heritage Travel: Top 10 Reasons According to Adoptees and Families," The Ties Program, www.adoptivefamilytravel.com.

"Yes, and..."

"Yes, and..." is a bedrock principle of improvisational comedy. It is about *accepting* what is before you in an improv sketch and working *with* it rather than trying to *obliterate or change* what is a given.

So what does this have to do with your life as an international adoptee? Actually a lot, when you think about all the issues and questions that present themselves on a regular basis.

Am I grateful, or angry?

Do I have a single, or a complex identity?

Who is most important to me, my adoptive family or my birth family?

Is adoption more of a net benefit, or loss?

Impossible choices! How do you choose between these options? Or better yet, *why* do these choices have to be made at all? Are these pairs truly opposites that snuff each other out, yielding only either/or answers?

The answer is a resounding *no*. Seemingly conflicting ideas co-exist simply because we are human beings. We all carry feelings and experiences that seem contradictory. One of the tasks of growing up is to discover our innate ability to embrace things that seem to be in opposition to each other, but which in reality just naturally occur together. And while we have the capacity to corral a whole range of emotions, thoughts, and experiences, it is also completely natural to crave consistency, predictability and streamlined ideas. Meanwhile, our brains actually *thrive* on varieties of thinking, feeling, and external challenges.

It is only through receiving information, support, and a heap of self-acceptance that we will be able—little by little—to weave all of these various threads into who we are becoming.

In other words, "YES, I experience this AND I also feel that."

GRATITUDE VS. ANGER AND GRIEF

If you've ever experienced anger or grief in connection with your adoption, does that mean you are an ingrate? And if you ever found the courage to express those emotions, did you resent being labeled an "angry adoptee," or some other negative tag? If so, did you then feel the need to defend and justify how grateful you truly are? Or to justify why you feel this anger or grief?

If you are appreciative most of the time, should this deny you the right to experience other emotions, like grief, anger, fear, confusion? Again, the answer is a resounding no. There are times when you feel *all* of these things: Angry, grateful, grieving—perhaps even neutral, when you need an emotional rest. In the words of one unnamed adoptee:

"At times, you may see a happy, well-adjusted adoptee. I may smile and laugh and hug and say, 'I love you–I'm so grateful to be adopted.' But inside, I am hiding deep pain, confusion, turmoil, grief and guilt...I cover it up so well that I forget that it's even there ...I convince myself that I feel nothing—other than what I am told to feel: Gratitude, joy, peace..."

WHO AM I? MAINSTREAM CULTURE VS. BIRTH CULTURE

"The privilege of a lifetime is being who you are."—Joseph Campbell

Our society often seeks to impose bold clear lines of racial and ethnic definition. But of course we know that many people are more layered than that. Maybe you are not sure what your particular mix might be—or perhaps it's not important to you. Either way, you don't need to be bound by the dictates of *other* people's comfort zones, which may demand clearly drawn racial or ethnic portraits: "Are you this, or that? You *must* be one of them."

The answer, quite frankly, is more like: "No, not necessarily. And, besides, I don't owe anyone a definition of myself."

Which group or culture is the place of true belonging? The confusion can be real and painful. No doubt mainstream culture of the United States is probably the most dominant cultural force you have been exposed to. In all likelihood you have not been nearly as immersed in your own birth culture's language, customs, arts, food, or religion. If you are culturally American, yet transracially/transnationally adopted, your own birth culture and country might not feel like a natural fit. Yet this was the world of your conception and birth, and so it may always be a powerful undercurrent in your life. Both identities are very real. One does not replace the other.

These two cultures—adopted and birth—need not compete for your loyalty, or your attention. You can embrace multiple cultures at the same time, as Jenni Fang Lee has experienced and vividly describes.[48] After all, your experience as an international adoptee has made you a global citizen.

∾

"I look Asian, but culturally I'm 'white'...I feel comfortable with that." Then, a little over one year later *"I no longer identify as white, but as Asian-American."* —Jesse

∾

"I went to the International House where there were all these people of color, and where there was also this student group, and people were proud to be people of color, and that was the first time I really

thought 'Oh, maybe it's okay to not be White.'

"Just because you take a detour from the main road doesn't mean you lose your identity."—KENNY

∽

Kenny went on to describe standing in front of the mirror as a kid and pushing his facial features around to imagine how he would look if he fit in with his community. But he also shared that after growing up, and witnessing the election of Barack Obama who is also biracial, made a huge difference to him. This helped him absorb the reality he needed, that he could be mixed race *and* also be widely acceptable.

ADOPTIVE FAMILY VS. BIRTH FAMILY

You are connected to (at least) two families: Your adoptive family, and your birth family. And although you may or may not know your biological family, they are still a part of you—in your DNA and likely in your imagination. This sense of connection with each family is your natural right, even if some feel threatened by your affections, or longings, for the other. This is not to say that there is anything simple about these feelings, only that they can co-exist inside you. As one adoptee put it:

∽

"Like those who have lost a parent through illness, or absentee-ism, I know I have an emotional burden of the uncertainty, hurt, and unfairness of the situation surrounding my birth parents and unknown history. But like many others, although I can't say I've found peace with the situation, I've come to terms with it as a part of my whole. Instead of covering the emotions over and pretending they're not there, I think I've learned to accept their existence and live alongside them."—AIMEE

~

"I have been given confidence by my fellow adoptees and by a welcoming Korean-American community. Their acceptance and guidance has slowly been fusing the gap between the person I was raised to be and the person I want to be. And, always, I will hover in the 'third space' with my fellow adoptees. We cling to each other as we each try to find our own balance."—SHELISE GIESEKE[49]

ADOPTION: NET LOSS, OR BENEFIT?

Some people maintain that any loss is unimportant compared to what children gain through adoption. But as many conversations with adoptees make clear, these losses and gains cannot be placed on the same scale. A child's right to love, safety, and security cannot be fairly compared to the loss of birth family and culture. Gains and losses exist side by side. This unfortunate "either/or" framing of the issue finds frequent expression in discussions of transracial adoption. As Michael Gerson—whose wife is a Korean adoptee—wrote in the *Washington Post*: "Ethnicity is an abstraction...Every culture or race is outweighed when the life of a child is placed on the other side of the balance."[50]

National Review writer and adoptive father David French utterly dismissed the use of the word "culture" in connection with internationally adopted children as "the culture of starvation, of rags, of disease, and of abandonment."[51]

In my view, the failure to acknowledge the impact of loss of family and birth culture that is imbedded in international adop-tion—a loss that has a continuing and pervasive impact for adoptees *and* birth families—does a great disservice to adoptees. Even as many wonderful opportunities become possible in the lives of inter-national adoptees with their adoptive families, these opportunities don't wipe away the losses and they cannot be fairly compared. Rather, they all come together in a single package. It is simply not possible to be adopted—even into the most loving, open-minded, and supportive family—and to escape the profound losses with which that adoption began.

Again, the words of Shelise Gieseke:
"Even though it is often downplayed or ignored, I am an Asian immigrant who was sent as a baby to fend for myself in a land of strangers. A land where I could not be comforted by the sound of my language or filled with food cooked by my grandmother's hand; where I was raised to become a stranger to my own motherland... Where I once thought of adoption as a finite event and something I should 'get over,' I now acknowledge that adoption is a lifelong experience that will always be an influence on my life. I can confidently identify as a Korean adoptee. Something I was raised to be, but something different than my birthright." [52]

∽

Both loss and gain are embedded in the adoption experience and cannot be disentangled. One is just as real as the other. Although one may beg for more focus at any given moment, you will have the strength and the spaciousness to contain all the seemingly contradictory elements of your own history and emotional life. Grieving what is lost does not mean you fail to appreciate the good fortune you have gained. Actually the two are intimately connected, the grief making a fuller appreciation possible.

Your emotional world will sometimes be challenged—by friends, family, co-workers, media, teachers, and your own internal wrestling. But despite these challenges—and because of them—your capacity for self-acceptance will keep growing, along with the space you have for all those elements that seem to be in conflict, to exist together, side by side.

SHADES OF GRAY, BEAMS OF LIGHT

So this is the way it is now, the night descending with soft tambourine sounds of cicadas melding with frog calls like fingernails on zippers.

As Gina settled down on her sweat-slick sleeping pad in Belize and watched the moonbeams thread their way through the mosquito netting, it seemed to her that night was the best part of the day. A time when you could slow down enough to absorb it all, summon new sights from the dimming light, and tease new sounds out of the deepening darkness.

Tonight, for the first time, she noticed how the folds of mosquito netting gathered into the center way at the very top, which tipped her imagination toward something out of reach, like one of those dreams that slip through the cocoon of sleep and vaporize.

Actually, "vaporizing" was the sort of thing that only recently had appealed to her. Not as a trendy, smoke-driven activity, but something else altogether that would mercifully remove her from everything she had known.

Gina stretched her tired body, more than ready for sleep. As her eyes closed, she could see her life as if she had paused on a mountain trek and could look back over her shoulder on the miles of trail she had already traveled: From Guatemala where she was born; to Colleyville, Texas, where her adoptive family lived; to Ohio State University where she used to be a junior Evolution and Ecology major/Botany minor. She still liked to define herself via her major, even silently in her head, even alone here at the edge of the jungle.

She had landed in Columbus, Ohio, a few years earlier with her accent streaming out ahead of her. She had tried—with mixed success—to shed her Texas talk because people there really did not expect someone with her brown ethnicity to emit that drawl. She was *so* tired of explaining that her life had begun in Guatemala, and then having to endure the polite "Ohhh, interesting," all too often accompanied by that flicker in the eyes of even more questions, which would send her spinning away as if pivoted by an invisible dance partner.

Ever-fascinated by green and growing things, Gina had stuffed her small light-drenched room at home with plants, tropical and otherwise. She had trays for seedlings under grow lights, and tools for grafts and propagation. You could hardly see the paint on the walls for all the hanging and climbing vines. Her family referred to her room as the rain forest, which she minded a little, but said nothing about, and was careful not to over-think.

The family garden in their compact yard was inviting too, but despite her parents' strong encouragement to play in the dirt and develop a cultivated plot, she hesitated lest someone mistake her for a hired gardener. On rare occasions, she would venture out with her headlamp way after sunset to the side strip which was the main blank slate of earth next to the house, and transplant some starts from her room. Shame, and a sense of needing cover, were two of her earliest companions—even if she didn't name them.

For the nearly 19 years since she had landed in Colleyville with her adoptive parents, she had been obliged to explain herself. But it was in the Rust Belt that she had been ready to put all that explaining on hold, to escape everyone's curiosity, and just be seen "right here, right now."

At college, it was activism, not sorority life, that had tugged at her, and she had participated in the Powershift Network's

Ohio Student Environmental Coalition: "Stop coal and fracking. Transition to renewables and clean energy alternatives. Collaborate with voting rights activists." And it was this last one that held the juncture where Jase had made his presence so brightly known.

He was fairly cute. She'd been drawn to him from the beginning with his lanky body, steady eye contact, and mass of very curly brown hair framing pale cocoa skin. Bi-racial and also adopted, Jase had grown up in a diverse Boston neighborhood in a multi-racial, multi-cultural family. Coming to this campus with a spectrum of races and cultures had in no way unnerved him the way it had her. And, amazingly, he was the only other person she knew who liked cilantro. The perfect first real boyfriend.

Little rivers of sweat trickled from her armpits and pooled on the mat. The walls of heat pushed against her from every angle, intrusive and inescapable, transporting her back to the kitchen of the Ohio State cafeteria where she used to work stirring giant steaming pots of chili and boiling pasta.

Funny, it was still all so real. She could still feel the flat of her palm push through the doors of the cafeteria when it was time to start her shift and how her hands met at the small of her back when she tied her apron, then reached up to pull that stupid hairnet over her head.

But why bother with this now, in the middle of such a vastly different faraway world?

Gina had been secretly watchful as far back as she could remember. She had a talent for remembering things in great detail. But more than "things," it was humans she was searching out, and many a face had been captured on the pages of her sketchbook, in pencil or charcoal, curiously, always in gray and white. When her brother Milo was little, he used to ask why she didn't use the colored pencils he gave her or the rainbow of felt tip pens she got from their parents. "Oh, I will," she would say. But she never did.

In this current moment, Gina's fingertips grazed her sketch pad tucked inside the edge of the mosquito netting. She wondered if this would be one of the times she could sketch herself to sleep. She started to doze as the pencil rolled lazily out of her hand and hit the floor. That small noise, together with intruding images of the college cafeteria where she worked only a short time ago, jostled her awake, remembering the only thing that had made her kitchen job halfway entertaining.

And it was this: She had the ability to store in her memory detailed images of faces and shards of conversation from the flow of students and later record them in her sketch book. This was a talent that she privately savored.

What she tried hard *not* to savor (with little success) was the memory of a familiar voice that once, about a year ago, cut into the hum of dishes clattering inside the busy cafeteria.

"Hey, Hairnet, can I get a veggie burger with a side of nutritional yeast?"

"Get *outa* here, Jase!"

She could feel her face reddening as she struggled to keep her mouth from stretching into a smile. So she rolled her eyes, hoping that would be the only noticeable thing.

"Aw, c'mon, I love your outfit! Let's get together later on."

Gina shook her head, wobbling her pile of carelessly netted hair as she slapped some food on a plate and shoved it in his direction.

But Jase had only laughed, then tipped his baseball cap to her as he added "So that's a 'yes' then?"

Aargh—how could someone be so totally annoying *and* totally adorable at the same time? Or at least that's what she thought back then.

Although the campus was diverse, it was also weirdly socially segregated. Asians hung out with Asians, Whites with Whites, and

Blacks with Blacks. To be sure, there were some exceptions, but the last time she had joined Jase in the library where the African-American students congregated, they were suspicious of her. And indeed, after she had exited the library that afternoon, an exchange had taken place between Jase and a girl he barely knew.

"Hey, Jase—what was *she* doin' here? Lookin' for action?"

"Yeah, you got that right" he grinned, "with *me*."

Gina was amused and, okay, flattered when she heard that story. So Jase's take-away from that experience was that he had deflected that negative swipe with charm, and therefore had more firmly entrenched himself as her boyfriend. Her take-away, however, had the lingering taste of hurt via the unopposed message that being Latinx wasn't enough of a credential to be welcome, and in fact had made her an object of suspicion because she was racially "wrong."

"Why are you lookin' at me that way? C'mon, Gina. Lighten up, girl," he had said.

At that point, she had opted for a sudden left turn in the conversation.

"Milo is coming tomorrow, remember? Is it still okay for him to sleep on your couch? He's bringing his sleeping bag, and I have a pillow for him."

"Oh, yeah, totally cool. Lookin' forward to meeting your little bro."

"He's a great kid. Just a bit needy sometimes, that's all—at least where I'm concerned. Always looked up to me a lot, which makes me squirm. Now things are a bit rough in high school, and he's taking some days off to come visit, check out the campus…"

"…And his sister's boyfriend, I get it. An agent dispatched by Paul and Janet of Colleyville."

"Not exactly. It's not all about *you*. They give me a lot of rope, never hovered much. Which is why I turned out so perfect, unlike you my darling sociology major. By the way, where *are* you gonna go with that non-credential of yours??"

And at that, he had snatched his hat and swatted her with it, although it was impossible to make him really angry. God knows she'd been trying her hardest for the past eight months.

So maybe since she had failed to push him away with her occasional put downs, *she* had to be the one to run? But now, here in her cocoon, well-sheltered from the hungry mosquitoes, his presence was still so immediate she might as well have been in his apartment in that faded red brick building.

Gina's mind flashed back to that Thursday when she had been walking across campus, her eyes wondering at the dark cloud boulders above rimmed in light. She heard a text come through, and stumbled off a curb: *"Uhhhhhh... where the h r u??"*

"SO sorry, Mi!! Got tied up. See you in 20. DON'T MOVE!"

A major screw up.

When she wasn't tripping over curbs, Gina was usually a swift and efficient mover. Fortunately she arrived at the Union in exactly twenty-three minutes, panting and sheepish. There, sitting on a concrete wall, gray backpack at his feet and not about to budge to meet her halfway was her little brother, waiting as instructed.

When she spotted him, she ran over and leaned in for a hug. His right arm slung around her limply.

"I'm *so* glad you're here. Honestly!" Gina had said.

"You mean now that I've reminded you. What exactly were you tied up doing?"

"I was at the Research Lab."

"Research must be pretty intense then."

"Hey, can we drop it, please? I already apologized. I am truly, truly sorry."

"Sure," he said as he cautiously made his way toward being agreeable. But Milo didn't take kindly to being forgotten. Each experience that smacked of rejection had made an imprint in the wet clay of his psyche. In 16 years he had amassed quite a collection of these.

They hopped a shuttle to the north end of campus and walked three blocks to Jase's apartment—#422—with two roommates, three small bedrooms, and an ultra-slim kitchen.

The roomy old living room, painted bright yellow, contained a tattered red fold-out sofa, a coffee table with carved initials (found that way), an assortment of faded green plaid floor cushions, and a stray chair. The blinds were up, and you could see an elm tree outside whose golden leaves filled its spreading arms. As Milo dumped his backpack on the floor, they looked out the window together.

"See?" Gina said. "You don't even need to lower the blinds. Not like home with nosey neighbors on all sides. Cool, huh?"

"So. You have a key to his apartment? Where is he anyway? Welcome committee away on vacation or something?"

"He's on his way, Milo. I thought you were gonna let this go. Jase is really psyched to meet you. Trust me, the place is never this clean, and it usually smells heavily of popcorn, ramen noodles... and other things."

Hearing a key in the door, Gina sang out "It's open!" and Jase came in.

"Hey, Milo. Nice to meet you," Jase said as he extended his hand in Milo's direction with a warm, wide-mouthed grin. Milo stopped short of a return smile, but shook his hand with a quick release. Whereas Jase's lanky form was edging past six feet in height, Milo was barely five-foot-nine and stocky. Normally, he would have been intimidated by a much taller guy, but somehow he didn't have that reaction here.

As Jase wrapped his arm around Gina, he asked her, "So how'd you get your hands on my apartment key? I notice I don't have your key."

At that, she had punched him in the shoulder, and then leaned her head against it as she slipped a key into his open palm. Milo watched with curiosity.

"Hey, is anybody hungry?" Gina asked.

They trooped over to her place, not too far away, a big old off-campus apartment she shared with three other students. They shared cooking and clean-up duties, which helped save time, energy, and was easier on the budgets.

Mounds of pasta primavera and heaps of green salad awaited, with double chocolate chip cookies for dessert. She chipped in money for her two guests, and wondered how she was going to create some linkage—or at least some ease—between the two guys. All three seemed to have a stake in this, yet she felt it was on her to make it happen. The problem was that she didn't really see how her brother and her boyfriend had much in common, besides their connection to her. Although they were both adopted, that didn't seem like enough to forge a relationship, she thought. At least between her and Jase, the subject rarely came up.

Thinking about how to manage this awkwardness was exhausting. If only this were Sunday, and she were putting Milo back on the shuttle to the airport!

Fortunately, dinner was a sort of merry distraction.

Haley was naturally gregarious, and in fine form. "Milo! Great to meet you. Grab a plate and dig in. I made the sauce. Let me know if you like it. Really—be honest now!"

Milo mustered a smile and tasted his first forkful, then gave it a thumbs up to scattered applause. Grant—tall, blonde, of mid-west farm stock—said "Haley's made this a thousand times. She didn't tell you that part. It's her signature dish. Lots and lots of practice. On the other hand, I made the pasta for the first time. Outstanding, right?"

Milo nodded in agreement. All he had to do so far was move

his head up and down and flip his thumb in the air. This social-
izing wasn't half as arduous as he expected, but he was ready for
the focus to switch to someone else. So far, college life seemed
a lot like the high school life he was used to, minus the accents.
Looking around this table of eight, he noticed that only he, Gina,
and Jase brought in the diversity factor. Otherwise, it was just like
Colleyville, an expanse of whiteness.

Milo vaguely recalled Gina complaining about a girl named
Shannon, very recognizable as the tallest female in the room, with
long brown hair and a smattering of freckles. As if on cue, she
jumped in with a real conversation starter.

"So, it's really cool that you three are all adopted. It's so amazing
that you got to come to the U.S. from those poor countries. Where
are you from again?"

"The U.S." said Jase, deadpan.

"Oh, really?" said Shannon. "I always thought you were from
Haiti for some reason. Or some place in Africa."

"Nope." Jase offered nothing more.

Shannon was the perkiest runaway train ever. Taking no cue
whatsoever from Jase, she hurtled forward, turning toward Gina
and Milo. "Well, what about you guys? Are you, like, bio brother
and sister? From—I forget—Mexico?"

"No and no," said Gina, standing up. "Let's clear the table. It's
my night for dishes and I have to get moving. It's already 7:30."

Milo and Jase also rose to their feet and headed for the kitchen,
where they each nabbed a dish towel. Jase gave Gina a small squeeze
on the back of her neck as he stage-whispered, "No social graces
AT all. Sorry for the awkwardness, Milo man."

"Well, it's nothing compared to school actually."

Milo, who was hoping this would segue into the conversation he
had counted on having during this visit, looked disappointed when

Gina—who had been silently pushing suds around on a plate—finally responded. "You know, Mi, you'll get through it. Only this year and next, and you're free to exit Texas."

"I can count, too. Thanks, Gina."

"I guess he's looking for a bigger talk," Jase observed.

Gina turned around and glared in Jase's direction. "Okay. So I'm not the perfect sibling like you are, apparently. But we *all* go through stuff."

"Did I miss something? Like why you're picking a fight with me?"

"Fine. Never mind." Gina snatched the towel from each of them, then hung them on their hooks. She quickly hugged only Milo before saying "Have a good night, you guys." Then she hustled them out the door and only later heard how the conversation had rolled out.

"So, what's happening at school?" Jase had asked as they walked out the apartment door and crossed the threshold into the night.

"It just sucks, that's all. Gina's no better than mom and dad. Nobody gets it."

"There are a million reasons high school can suck. What's your version?"

"Oh, like girls, you know. Like who will go out with me if they can't see past my skin."

Milo shoved his hands in his jeans pockets, puffed out his cheeks, and blew into the cold air like he was making smoke rings.

"Yeah, I know," Jase answered. "That. Is. Tough."

"So do you *really* know how tough it is, everyone clumped up in the cafeteria everyday, and me just grabbing a sandwich and getting out of there as fast as I can? Did you ever go through that?"

"Not exactly like that," said Jase slowly. "I didn't live in a super whitewhite neighborhood. More like Joseph's Coat of Many Colors."

"So even *you* don't get it. Fantastic."

"Hey, your high school experience doesn't have to be twinsies with mine. It's not like I've never experienced rejection because of my race. Right here on this campus, as a matter of fact."

"Like what?"

"First year in the dorm. I was in a triple with two white dudes, instate students from small towns, never saw a black person in their lives. Then, bingo, now they're living with one. They used to go out and get hammered, then come back to the room and it would get ugly. I had to bring in reinforcements—first the brothers in the dorm, and then the uni police."

"How long did you stay in that situation?"

"Way too long. Two months of f–ing hell. Welcome to OSU."

"But you're still here. You didn't drop out, or transfer. Dropping out, that's what I want to do."

"Yeah, I know, I know. But you don't want to mess with your future. I have a scholarship here. Plus, I joined the Black Students Association and got instant community. But, wait: You never said what happened at Colleyville High that was so terrible to make you want to ditch it all."

By now, they had arrived at Jase's apartment building. The blinds were up, and you could see people inside appearing through the branches. One of them might have been a girl.

"You live with *girls*?" Milo asked, trying to sound casual while his nervousness started idling.

"Yeah. But just one. Don't freak out, man," laughed Jase. "It's bedtime anyway—or we'll force the issue, so you can have the living room."

He turned the key and walked in first. There was Aisha, with James right behind her. Introductions without handshakes this time, just nods.

"Milo's sleeping there on the couch," Jase reminded them. "Soon."

"You're good, you're good," said Aisha. "We're heading for bed in five minutes, promise—right James?"

"Mmm hmm," said James, looking straight ahead.

Jase checked his phone. Nothing from Gina. He wasn't going to be the first to do repair-texting.

"So, Milo, you want something to drink?"

"Sure. What d'you got?"

Jase opened the refrigerator. "Orange juice, milk, coffee, wine, tea and…" with a grand gesture toward the faucet, "…water. But you're not going to sleep till you fill out the school details. Sure you don't want coffee?? I'm gonna keep you up."

Milo's face suddenly opened into a broad smile. "Ok fine. But I'll take the juice without the caffeine."

"Fair enough."

Juice poured, they sat down on wooden chairs with chipped red and blue paint. The table tilted back and forth between them depending on whose elbows were drilling in.

"So what's our topic," demanded Jase nicely enough. "Racial issues? Girls? Adoption? All of the above?"

"Do you and Gina ever talk about this stuff? I can't get her to talk to me. Or listen, for that matter."

"Yeah, she's pretty buttoned up in that way. That girl will chat about anything, as long as you don't make it too personal. Then she finds a way to evaporate, *fast*. Poof. Gone."

Which is the way the night went. Minutes and hours swiftly carried away by conversation that had been on hold for years of Milo's life.

It was somewhere around four a.m. when they decided to catch some sleep. "To be continued," Jase yawned patting Milo on the shoulder seconds before he fell onto the couch without bothering to unfold it.

For Gina, on the other hand, the night had slowly crawled by. Hours after Milo's and Jase's departure, Gina wandered into the kitchen to grab some milk. She grabbed the carton and the face of a missing child flashed before her eyes. Why hadn't this popped out at her before now? The carton went back in the fridge and she opted for a glass of water instead. Haley was there and looked up from her laptop propped on the kitchen table. "Hey, Gina. What's up?"

"Oh, nothing. See you tomorrow," came Gina's gray-voiced response.

"All right, then." Haley, eyes widening a bit. She hesitated a moment before returning to her screen.

Gina went to her plant-free room, and closed the door. Who had time for low light cultivation in this tiny space? She couldn't bear it when plants faltered and died, so in this environment she didn't even want to try. Not even with a philodendron.

She flipped open her laptop and tried to divert her agitation into productive study time. Couldn't do it. She tried watching reruns of "Arrested Development," but nothing seemed remotely amusing, all about as interesting as shredded wheat. She grabbed her jacket and headed out for a walk in the neighborhood. By now it was two a.m. and this was against her better judgment—which wasn't flexing much muscle at the moment. As she checked her empty phone over and over again, her stride was long and brisk. After a small branch jumped across her face, she ripped at it impatiently, twisting it until it broke. She looked at the jagged edge of greenness with a pang of regret, vowing to come back and fix it tomorrow with a clean diagonal cut.

But in no time, she was fuming again. At Jase for forging an alliance with her brother. At Milo for giving him that opportunity. She felt wrongfully excluded. There was no way she was calling either of them in the morning.

"I can't keep wandering around out here," Gina muttered out loud to herself. Then, catching the eye of a lone guy in a torn sweatshirt leaning against a building, she made an abrupt about face and headed for home.

Morning eventually came after Gina had slept poorly, the phone buzzing her awake. Through a drowsy fog her eyes and brain began to grope for each other.

"Meet 4 breakfast/lunch??"

Milo, not Jase. Whoa—12:30!!

"Diving into clothes right now—See you @ Birdie's?"

She hoped Milo would show up alone. She also hoped he wouldn't. Feeling irritated with herself, she still managed to comb her hair carefully. Ponytail, copper spiral earrings from the craft fair. She picked up her mascara and leaned into the mirror but abruptly turned and threw it back in the bag. "Hell with it."

When Gina arrived at Birdie's, she shoved the door with such force it flew away from her, banging into the front wall.

"Oh sorry, sorry!" she said, realizing there was an elderly man in her path.

"Barely survived that one," he said calmly. "At least I hung on to my hat."

Gina smiled in the face of kindness she was not sure she deserved. Milo waved from a window table. She felt both relieved, and wounded, that he was indeed alone.

"Good afternoon," he said brightly. "How's it goin'?"

"Not bad. And you?" Gina began perusing the menu.

"Really good. Jase and I talked basically all night. He's a pretty cool guy."

That didn't take long. Gina's stomach clenched.

"Yeah," she managed to say in a measured tone before quickly looping around to the menu. "You want to split the green omelette? Portions are massive here."

"Sure. Sounds great."

After they had ordered, Milo broke the silence with a question.

"So, you want to hear about our conversation?"

She didn't, but managed to reply calmly. "Sure. Fire away."

"I don't know. Somehow you don't seem to care."

"No, Mi, that's not true. It's just I've heard it all before. I know high school can suck. You'll get through it. We all do. Whether we're brown or yellow or black."

"Or adopted."

"Yeah, that too."

The giant, steaming omelette quickly arrived stuffed with spinach, avocado, scallions, and the extra cilantro Gina had requested. Potatoes tinged with turmeric were heaped on the side with a mound of greens topped with shaved beets.

After Gina deftly scooped her portion onto the empty plate the server had provided, she pushed the remainder across the table to Milo. There was a glare through the window making it hard for her to focus on him without squinting—a perfect excuse to focus exclusively on the eggs.

"We could move..." said Milo.

"...Except this is the only two-top left," finished Gina. "Why don't we just lower the shade. That'll help."

She continued to gaze at her plate as if it were thousands of miles away, while picking steadily at her food.

"So how much do you know about Jase's family? Since it seems like you guys don't talk that much," he said.

"Is that what he told you? Well, that's great. Guess he's trying to shove me aside and gain a brother in the process. Nice move."

Milo ignored the retort. "He has two sisters, one biological and one adopted. He's actually more connected to his bio sister and..."

"Tell me something I don't know," Gina fired back. "What's your point anyway?"

"That there is a lot of resentment between him and the younger sister adopted from India. Because Jase was adopted three days after he was born. And he's met his birth family. And Nita was fifteen months old at adoption, with zero information about her birth family."

"Got it. Now tell me your point."

"Jesus, what is the matter with you, Gina? Can't we have a real conversation without you shooting bullets at me? Jase actually *listened.* We went back and forth, sharing stuff, asking questions. Pretty simple, actually. Why can't *you* do that? Is it because you're jealous of me, like Nita is of Jase, or what?"

Gina smashed the table between them, then looked around. Lots of eyes rolled in their direction.

"*No.* I am *not* jealous of you," she hissed hoping to get her younger brother to cease and desist.

"You and Jase just carry on and on and on with your deep conversations. Enjoy yourselves and your fabulous new friendship. I have better things to do than delve into things I can't change, you can't change, and even our hero Jase can't do anything about. And now—I gotta go."

She grabbed her jacket and bag and rushed out the door, leaving half her meal behind. Five seconds later, she blew back through the door. "Sorry," she muttered, "I still have to pay this stupid bill."

Outside, the wind was picking up as she trudged to the Research Lab through swirls of dead leaves laced with snack bar wrappers and flyers advertising meetings and special deals. "What a mistake to have him visit. Everything was fine till he showed up, and now..." But in less than a minute, her anger dissolved, and she found herself wading in guilt. "All right. I'll text him later. Or maybe now."

She clicked out a brief apology, and pressed "Send." Followed by a large exhale. Now she could relax.

After entering the building, she crammed her stuff in the cabinet and proceeded to the lab, where she signed in, then meandered to the backroom with all the grow lights and seedlings. Shelf after shelf of tiny green forms striving, leaves and shoots pushing toward the light, roots forging their minute, unseen pathways in the dark. Closing her eyes, she felt her lungs rise and widen to make room for a large intake of this delicious, earthy air.

On the back shelf were trays of seeds waiting to be identified by phenotype. Gina donned her blue gloves, enjoying the way they made her feel official, like she actually belonged in this place instead of just being a lowly volunteer working for academic credit. But, in another way, the gloves felt confining, a layer of numbness, dulling that sense of tender leaves and velvety soil meeting her fingertips.

She stood still, tugging on first the right, then the left, then the right glove again.

"I think you finally got a perfect fit there, Regina." She was unaware that Matt, the grad student lab manager had been standing there watching her with curiosity.

"Oh, hi Matt," she said. "Where did you come from? I had no idea you were lurking nearby."

"Yeah, we grad students are highly skilled lurkers. Just not highly paid." His eyes smiled behind his glasses. She smiled faintly back.

"You okay?" he asked.

"Oh yeah, sure. Just a little sleep deprived." She looked around the room and saw it as a whole landscape for the first time—not plant, plant, plant, in plastic pots or jars with foil lids, but drifts of young bright green, delicate leaves, pointy, feathery, or oval, some open flat, some slowly revealing themselves as they unfurled in their own tempo. She could feel the life force pulsing in this room, as if it were humming with tiny heartbeats.

Matt was still standing there.

"Guess I better get back to work," he said, touching her elbow lightly. "Take care."

"Yeah, thanks, Matt." She glanced at him quickly, and as soon as he turned away, her eyes filled. Matt had quietly offered her some kindness that she couldn't seem to summon for herself. She squeezed her eyes shut, forcing tears down her cheeks, and stood motionless as she attempted to calm herself before she allowed them to open again. Her blurry gaze roved over this controlled environment with its precisely measured containers, carefully adjusted grow lights, perfectly modulated temperatures—and these garish gloves. She felt ill.

Suddenly, Gina tore off the gloves, threw them in the special trash bin, and erased her name from the time sheet. With a sideways glance at the bulletin board, she caught the letters WWW for an instant, then hustled out the door and headed home in a storm of confusion. Twenty minutes later, arriving with no memory of how she had gotten there, she saw a familiar form leaning against her building.

"Gina, can we just talk?"

"Jase, not now. I'm on my way to the gym. How about after that?"

"You don't seem like yourself."

"Well, maybe that's true, I don't know. Can we just hold off? I don't even know what to say right now."

"How about that you still care about me?"

"I don't know what I feel about anything. Or anyone!"

After this outburst, through tears swarming into her eyes, she saw a cloud descend on Jase and immediately regretted her words.

"Oh, I'm sorry! I...I didn't actually mean what you're thinking. I'm just a wreck, that's all."

"From what exactly?" He was genuinely baffled. "I've never seen you like this before. How did you get so...so...unhinged?"

"I don't know. I just don't know."

Suddenly, Jase seemed large, bulky and menacing, as if he had pulled a rip cord releasing a snarling, snapping animal who had been kept fenced in for the months she had known him. This was a creature totally unfamiliar to her.

"WELL, THAT'S NOT GOOD ENOUGH," he yelled. "I'm tired of your excuses. Your brother comes to see you for a few days, and you're a total brat for no reason. And all you can come up with is 'I don't know?'"

"Oh, so this is about Milo now? Nice that he finally found his BFF, his confidante, and his warrior hero all in one! I s'pose you've already bestowed him with all the answers he needs about school and adoption and race relations. How cool are *you*?!?"

"WHAT?! Like you never really thought about any of these things before? Really, Gina?! Nobody believes that. Not even *you*." Jase jutted his chin forward and grabbed her arm to stress his point.

"Don't touch me," she spat out, shaking herself loose of him. She was reeling, cornered, all her warning lights flashing. Feeling dizzy, wildly casting about for an exit, words escaped her. She turned and walked away, willing her feet to strike the ground and lead her anywhere but here with this new and nasty stranger. Maybe she had actually never really known Jase—or anyone else for that matter.

• • •

Now, under the folds of the mosquito net in Belize, those

memories were like a tourniquet around her that wouldn't release...
As a stray mosquito hovered over Gina, she assumed it was on the
other side of the net whining with hunger—until she felt a sting,
smacked her forehead and then smeared blood on her sketchpad.
Tomorrow this would be the foundation of an otherwise gray drawing, but for now she had to feed her mind other images, ones that
would invite her to sleep—like richly dark furrowed fields and
bright green seedlings. Like the faces of the two kids who had
shown up to volunteer the other day. They were probably part of
Tino's large extended family. Tino was the indispensable farm
handyman. Today she would make a point of learning the children's names.

Dawn seemed to arrive in a hurry. Gina parted the netting,
got up and threw some clothes on. She wandered into the commu-
nal kitchen, fried an egg, grabbed a small delectable banana, and
downed a cup of café con leche. After scrubbing the pan and spat-
ula, she washed her cup and ducked out to the cold frame, where,
hanging out by the door—bright and early—were the two kids,
watching her expectantly.

"Hola," Gina said. She turned her finger toward herself. "Soy
Gina, as they call me here. Y tu?" She then reversed her gesture
toward them.

With embarrassment, she realized that English or Spanish
might not be their mother tongue, although both were spoken by
the people of Belize. She could not assume they went to school,
where these languages would be taught. Maybe they spoke Mayan,
Kriol, or Garifuna. She knew nothing of their family life or origins.
And while she might appear to be from this part of the world, her
cultural lens was so American. So *white* American.

"I am Martin. She is Rubi," said the dimpled boy with the serious gaze. His eyebrows slanted down on the outer edges, which

made his studious look all the more compelling. His hair was cut ultra-short. She was tempted to stroke the fuzzy surface, but restrained herself. Instead, she smiled, and surrendered to English.

"You are brother and sister?"

"Yes," Martin said. "I am eleven. Rubi is eight."

Rubi had been looking pointedly away the whole time, but gradually turned to watch Gina. Her eyes, round and black, like lava rocks set in a perfect oval, peered out from under a green and white cap. Two very tiny crucifix earrings decorated her earlobes, a blessing gift, Gina imagined with some certainty, from her mother when she was baptized.

"I've seen you here before," said Gina. "Are you Tino's kids?"

Tino was always busy repairing something here—the chicken coop, the fences, the pick-up truck. She had no doubt the answer to her question was yes.

"No," Martin answered simply, somberly.

When no follow-up question came to mind, Gina moved on. "Well, come on then. Let's go check the bananas before the sun gets too high, okay?"

Wordlessly, they followed her into the orchard toward a clump of banana plants.

"You see how they like to grow close to each other for shade and shelter? Just like you and Martin." But the children continued to look ahead with no apparent reaction.

Then, Gina grabbed Rubi's hand and led the three of them under the large floppy leaves where there were clusters of bananas ready for picking. Rubi smiled mechanically for a fleeting instant.

Gina noticed that Rubi and her brother did not actually look alike. If it weren't for the identical asymmetric dimples—high under the cheekbone on the right, low above the jawline on the left. Other than this and the fact that they seemed inseparable, you would never assume they were related.

The children rapidly filled a nearby basket with ripe fruit, pulling off the dead leaves and suckers before hauling over a hose from nearby rainwater barrels to spray the thirsty banana leaves. Somehow they appeared to know what they were doing.

"You guys are good!" Gina noted, without drawing any conclusions as to how they had acquired these skills. "Here—I want to show you something funny."

They made their way into the center of the clump of trees where there was a vertical pipe, a showerhead, and a rubber mat.

Martin turned the faucet and water spurted out. "For the bananas," he asserted without surprise.

"Well, yes, and no," said Gina. "For us *and* the bananas. We get clean, and the bananas get more moisture."

He nodded his head. "They get thirsty and they get lonely."

"And hungry, too," Gina said. "By the way, did you guys have breakfast? At least the banana plants had chicken manure! And we'll give them more—lunch!"

It was okay that they didn't appreciate her pale jokes, but she didn't know what to do with all this silence. She picked a couple of bananas, offered them to the children. After a fifteen second hesitation, Martin accepted for both of them, at which point a vibrating hum caught their attention.

Gina pointed at a banana flower being probed by a violet and royal blue hummingbird with its pulsing throat of chartreuse. Rubi's eyes brightened as she looked up at Gina, and together they watched as this amazing little bird fluttered its wings so fast you couldn't see them. And, being a hummingbird, it could fly backwards. This was turning into a great morning.

"It takes about nine months for a plant to grow up and produce a bunch of bananas," explained Gina, settling happily into her role as a teacher. "Then the mother plant dies and..." but as she noticed their faces and the stories written there, she laid down the rest of her sentence and did not pick it up again.

They spent the rest of the morning quietly tending the banana trees, bringing wheelbarrows of chicken manure and mulch to spread on top. The children needed little instruction, or modeling of any kind, which made Gina curious. "So how did you guys get to be such experts? Expertos?"

Martin answered blandly, "We have done this before."

"Yes, I can see that." But Gina did not press him further.

When they were finished nourishing the bananas, Martin announced that it was time for them to leave. Gina was disappointed, hoping to make more of a connection over lunch by showing them her little sleeping alcove and some of her sketches.

"Thanks so much for your help."

"See you Jueves," Martin said, allowing his gaze to meet hers for a handful of seconds before the two headed for the gate.

Gina called after them, with a smattering of desperation in her voice thinly veiled in her casual offer. "Hey, you guys need a ride?"

"No, gracias" Martin responded, looking straight ahead down the road. Only Rubi turned and waved with her small slender arm at half-mast.

Suddenly, Gina was brimming with emptiness. She felt as if she herself was fading like an old photo as the children gradually disappeared at the bend of the road. For awhile she kept her eyes trained on the gate, waiting for it to sway open again with their return. Ultimately she decided that this feeling of gnawing emptiness might simply be a hunger for actual food so she headed for the kitchen.

Her boot-clad feet clunked up the two steps. She grabbed a tin plate from the drainer, then examined a frying pan on top of the hotplate and wondered if she was the only one who thought it a good idea to clean the pan between uses. Sighing, she reached for the steel wool, and scrubbed off the latest batch of beans, rice, and onions. After rinsing the pan, she flung the murky water outside, poured in some oil, and heated up those same ingredients for her own lunch.

Finally, Gina sat down on the bench facing the doorway that framed a scrubby dirt yard containing a single paduak tree, whose clusters of "wing fruit" dangled from the branches. She was very fond of these particular seed pods whose unique shape—like fanciful little hats—sheltered the potential beginnings of a new life.

A new life. A mere six weeks ago, something unknown within her had exploded, spinning her around and then spitting her out here in Central America near the land where her own roots had tried, but failed, to establish themselves.

Gina remembered that horrible day with Milo and Jase, when she had rushed past the lab bulletin board and a flyer had caught her eye, but she hadn't lingered long enough to absorb what it said.

An hour later, still agitated, she felt drawn back to the lab in order to read the rest of the ad: "Agricurious? Travel restless? Organic farm interns needed..."

It was at this point that she plopped right down on the wooden bench below the bulletin board and launched a frenetic Google search. Five days later, much to her own surprise, she was on a plane heading south via Miami to Belize.

Not one other person she knew had approved. Not family, not friends, not professors. Shocking, what she was capable of in the face of zero support: A sudden, and—to her, at least—delicious disappearance from the campus, and the country.

Milo had returned to Colleyville following an uneasy truce between them, but she hadn't gotten that far with Jase. She hated being pushed. He hated being pushed away. And it seemed as if a big obstacle had suddenly emerged between them. She could not see around it, and did not want to try, although Jase asked her questions that probed her heart and her memory.

"Why won't you think and talk about these things?"

"Because they are NOT important to me!" She had insisted this in such a loud voice that a couple walking hand-in-hand had stared pointedly in their direction.

"Did you ever consider that you refuse to think about stuff just maybe because it *is* very important to you?"

"Oh thanks. I wanted a boyfriend, not a shrink."

"Well, looks like you got neither. Proud of yourself??" Suddenly pivoting, he had walked away, his long legs carrying him swiftly toward the back of the Student Union. Too angry to stand still, Gina had quickly flipped herself around, and left the scene as well. Passively watching him disappear was *not* an option.

She wrote him a note before she took off for Belize. Three notes, actually.

First: "Your stuff is in a box at my place. Call Haley and arrange to pick it up. Thanks."

Then: "Taking leave for Belize. I'm sure I'll be more able to talk when I'm back in two months. If you still want to."

And, finally, a wavy white rectangle on a stick with one word. "*Truce*." Just that, no contact information.

In the end, Gina wanted to vanish without a word, so the notes came with her, never sent but never shredded.

But she did want to heal their rift. If only Jase could have a window into her storm-tossed heart, which she kept walled off without even realizing it. She now considered sending him all three notes, leaving him to sort them out and read them in whatever order.

Gina picked at her food and watched the flies buzz around her plate. Maybe she wasn't hungry after all. Just then a water bottle smacked down on the table, jumping her fork and springing her out of the endless loop of thoughts going nowhere.

"Whoops, Gina. Didn't really mean to scare you there."

"Oh, no! It's ok. Just thinking. How's it goin', Julia?"

"Fine, I guess. Been working on the yams and ginger roots today, digging them out of the compost for replanting. Garlic too. Very fun...at least until I realized the heat might kill me. It's a lot warmer than Vermont, for sure. How was your morning?"

"Good, good. Rubi and Martin and I took care of the banana trees. I really like them. Do you know anything about them? How do they end up here? They seem, I don't know, sort of secretive. Whose kids are they?"

Julia took a large slug of water. "There's no way to know that."

"What do you mean?"

"Well, they just come here from up the road."

Gina felt a new layer of sweat coating her skin. Up the road was the Paradiso, which was a working farm and home for abused and neglected kids. Other interns volunteered there, reading to the young ones, playing basketball with the older ones—both things Gina would normally enjoy, yet she always made excuses not to do. *So I guess those children found a way to come to me instead.*

Julia was watching her reaction. "Hey, I didn't mean to upset you or anything."

"Oh no, it's just that...they kind of won my heart, and I wanted to think of them as having a loving family. It's so disappointing. But it does explain some things."

"Like what?"

"Oh, like how they were so skilled with all the tasks I gave them: Harvesting and fertilizing, mulching and pruning. Basically everything we did, without a hitch, no questions asked. But shared nothing about their background. Now I get it."

"Well, there's actually more to it than that. You might be wondering how they landed at Paradiso?"

"Yeah, okay..."

"You may know that child labor is a big problem in Belize?"

"No, not really."

"Gina, where've you been? It's not just about coming here to practice permaculture, is it? You must have been at least slightly curious about the social environment?"

Gina absorbed the reprimand in silence.

"Rubi and Martin were rescued from a farm where their father had placed them to work and earn their school fees. Their mom died when Rubi was four, and he couldn't take care of them or afford school for both kids, so he put them on some huge banana and citrus farm. Martin was working fourteen-hour days. Sex traffickers were all around, and children were disappearing. Martin begged his father to at least transfer Rubi to a safe place, but he was not interested. By a stroke of luck, their maternal grandmother got wind of the situation and swiped the children one night with the help of a couple of staff members from Paradiso. So, yes, they've been rescued, but they've been traumatized. They won't trust you that easily, even if you think they should."

The story pumped through her bloodstream. Gina swallowed hard, fighting for self-control. She could feel Julia's gaze adhering to her and a moment later her composure split into a thousand pieces. She bent her face into her hands and tears poured into them.

"Oh, Gina," Julia said, scooting her chair closer and leaning in. "It's okay, it's okay. They're fine now. Really!"

Gina nodded mutely She turned the neck of her t-shirt inside out to blot her cheeks. The fabric was rough and unwelcome, reddening her skin in exchange for drying it.

Julia just kept watching her. While her gray eyes were not unfriendly, they were making Gina uncomfortable. She had nothing to say, nothing more to ask, and she wanted the conversation to end. She rose to her feet and firmly fixed her semi-shredded straw hat back on her head.

"Come up there with us sometime—you know, to Paradiso— and see for yourself," urged Julia softly.

"Yeah, maybe. But right now, I'm going into town. Need anything?" Her voice was still raspy. Julia shook her head.

"Ok. Well, so long. Enjoy your siesta. Well-earned, I'm guessing." She almost managed to smile.

Gina strode briskly to the gate and grabbed the bike that was leaning there. After a quick adjustment of her fanny pack, she was off down the dirt road to town. Julia, left standing on the step of the kitchen shack, was a little confused about Gina's sudden retreat. What was she running from? *We were just talking...*

Gina was actually just as bewildered herself. Why had she come here anyway? To escape Jase? Have a learning adventure in Belize? She had been drawn to it as a relatively peaceful and progressive Central American country, with its growing organic farm movement and high literacy rate, only to find out that it was plagued by sex trafficking and child labor violations. *And orphans.* It seemed they were everywhere. Or *we* were everywhere.

She pedaled on, guesstimating one and half miles to go to the store. Giving up on her hat, she let it dangle from her chin strap, the stray straws scratching her skin over and over with each pucker in the road. But there was no denying it was a beautiful ride. She loved the color contrasts, the bright green landscape against the light brown dust of the road, the palest of gray clouds backed by a brilliant blue sky. The houses, some with thatched grass roofs, others topped with rusty corrugated metal, were mostly on stilts, warped by moisture and leaning uncertainly.

Gina stopped, swung off her bike, and propped it against a tree. From underneath its branches she photographed the houses painted yellow and mint green, the ribbon of sea in the distance. Shouts behind her tugged her attention around to children splashing in a pond while their mothers, hair pinned high, sat at the edge, their weary feet as well as their toddlers soaking in the water. Gina worried the water might be polluted—actually, she was sure the water was polluted—and briefly considered approaching the mothers. Instead, she took more pictures.

She clicked through the photos as she walked back to the bike and she was amazed at how peaceful they looked, how they seemed to capture a life that was idyllic, lacking nothing. How easy it was to capture the undisturbed surface of things. Yet there was the creeping realization that this is not what she had come here to do.

She ducked under the palm, grateful for the shade on what must have been at least 100° day. The mere concept of that number launched another river of sweat running down the sides of her ribs. As she looked up at the sheltering fronds forming wedges of light that spilled down in front of her onto the warm, brown earth, she realized that both she and this tree preferred their solitary growth habits. It was good to be seen by another living being, especially one who was unable to speak.

Gina relaxed against the tree trunk and felt it highlight the small bones of her spine. Slowly reaching for her pack, she fished for her sketch pad and pencil stub, then flipped pages until she found a blank one. But as her pencil trailed tentatively on the paper, she wondered how to get the image of light to flow out of the point of blunt gray lead.

Ten feet away, a young woman wrapped in a purple shawl,

bulging with the body of a sleeping infant, studied Gina. Her thin dark brows knit together as she waited patiently to be noticed. Gina tapped her pencil on the sketch pad, hoping it would unlock some idea for her, but instead the pencil mutely rolled to the ground. Seizing this opportunity to make herself known, the woman stepped forward, extending one arm draped in cocoa bean necklaces, mumbling something so quietly that Gina couldn't tell if it was Spanish or Q'eqchi'—the language of the Mayan people.

Instinctively, Gina extended her hand too. In a surreal moment, it looked as if these two hands might have been part of the same body. Disoriented for an instant, Gina agreed to buy two necklaces. The woman nodded, but continued to stand there even after Gina had paid her.

Gina thought: *She obviously knows I'm a foreigner, or she wouldn't have approached me with the necklaces. Our transaction is over. Why won't she leave?*

"Belize? Maya?" The young woman pointed at Gina, her eyebrows wringing together.

"I'm from the States," Gina replied, in English, to purposely bolster her national identity. "Student. Estudiante."

The woman, nodded as she broke eye contact, and glanced down at her baby.

She thinks I'm lying. Okay. Maybe I am.

Gina swatted away the fly parked on her cheekbone. "So how old are you?" she finally asked, "Cuantos años?"

"Dieciséis. Tu?" she questioned, eyes steady.

Gina got that the girl was sixteen, but somehow her mental circuits fried and she blanked on the Spanish word for twenty. Looking up at the sky as if the needed translation might emerge from a cloud, she was annoyed at how the young woman's curiosity made her so patient. Still she waited.

"Dieciseis tambien?"

Hey, I am NOT you.

But there was the prompt she was waiting for. "Umm...veinte."

"Ahhh" came the rolling tone as a knowing smile began to form. She patted her infant and raised her eyebrows, pointing in Gina's direction, whose attention had strayed momentarily.

Long pause. Then she shook her head emphatically and pushed her hands out between them as if staving off an intruder. "Me? Oh no no no no. No children."

The woman continued watching her.

Wow—never mind. I gotta get outa here. Gina tossed the necklaces around her neck, smiling fast and trying to wave goodbye as she mounted the bike—a move that didn't work out all that smoothly. The front wheel wobbled left and right as she gripped the bars to get the bike under her control, and about 25 feet down the road she found herself circling back. *I can't believe this!* Her pack was still under the tree where she had tossed it. The young woman watched her, rooted to her spot in the shade.

Without a either a word or a wave this time, Gina took off again in the direction of the ruffling blue sea. Lightheadedness saturated her, and she was not altogether confident that she could apply the brakes before the dock's edge.

She plunged off the bike and landed hard on her feet, the strands of cocoa beans whipping against her. Confusion carted her thinking away, and her heart was pressed into a small wad. *What am I doing here? I could be farming in New Zealand, for God's sake.*

She watched the rhythmic churning of the waves. Maybe if she kept her eyes glued long enough the water would offer up a new answer, something besides her familiar mantra "just keep moving." But a sliver of thought slowly pushed in: *Moving isn't just away. It's also toward.* Okay—duh; but why hadn't this brilliance occurred to her before?

She could hear Jase's voice as if he were inches from her ear: "I don't get it. Why don't you even ask yourself a few *basic* questions?"

As she dug her fingernail into the flesh of her thumb, it felt good to remember why she hated him.

The water in her bottle was now hot enough to brew tea. She slurped some anyway, hoping to steady herself. Wheeling the bike over to the dockside grocery, she bought a sack of rice and headed back to the farm.

The breeze was hot and welcome, and she was relieved to be pedaling again. The added weight of the rice caused her to push harder. She could feel her strength returning and with her strength her balance.

It was late afternoon when Gina got back to the farm. The gate was open, and she looped her leg over the bike and propped it against the fence. The place looked deserted, empty of energy, but she knew otherwise. As long as she could remember, Gina had possessed the ability to sense within their silence the life force of green and growing things. This intuitive ability was one of her closely guarded secrets. Imagining being teased about it was not worth the risk.

All around her was brilliant green lushness. The air clung with what felt like the weight of moist, warm cloths. She flashed on the weird parallel world she had just come from—the late fall of Ohio, where deciduous trees and shrubs seem so devoid of vitality, while almost everything about them pulsed below the surface unobserved, or even minimally considered. To be perfectly honest, she felt just like one of those Ohio plants.

Gina curbed these thoughts and walked to the kitchen, tossed the bag of rice on the counter, then ambled over to her sleeping shack and up the two steps. She opened the rickety door with one finger and skidded in on something underfoot She looked down at a white envelope—and her heart lifted. A message from Jase! But although there was no return address on the front, she quickly recognized the handwriting. It belonged to her mother.

Disappointed despite herself, she plopped down hard on the cot's edge. Well, in a way this was a relief, she thought, easier to respond to Janet, who would probably write something newsy. She calmly opened the envelope, and slowly unfolded the blue graph paper that her mother was so attached to for some reason. Maybe she just liked all those little blue boxes that created a hoped-for sense of order. Just a theory.

• • •

Dear Gina,

We haven't heard from you since you announced your plans to take a leave from school for an experience in Belize. We have to respect your explanation, however vague, but would of course like to know how you are, so please write back. Thanks in advance. And a note to Milo would be great, too. He is still upset about his visit with you, and the ruptures that followed. Please don't break off your ties with him. He doesn't deserve that.

Otherwise, all is well here. Work is work and school is school. The Backman's tree keeled over in a storm and missed our bedroom by about three and half feet. That's the best news so far, and enough drama for awhile. You know I'm not that great with drama. :)

I am not sure what occupies your mind and heart while you're in Belize, but your journey has rekindled our own journey to that part of the world nineteen years ago, and there is something I'd like you to know. Although we were never given a copy of your birth mother's picture at the time of your adoption, as some families were, I did find out that the sealed envelope we had to surrender to immigration before we brought you home might have contained her photo. If you are so moved, you can contact U.S. Customs and Immigration (you can apply online) and retrieve copies of whatever was in that envelope. I encourage you to try this.

By the way, if you want company for a trip to Guatemala City, I'm up for it.

Sending love straight to you, no detours,
Mom

. . .

Gina read and re-read the letter, throat knotted, hands trembling, pages rattling as softly as a murmur. It felt like a current of air had suddenly intruded on the dense stillness of the room, driving her molecules apart.

Her mother had had so many extraneous words littering the landscape of family life all these years that "real" conversations had been sparse. Usually, Gina had thought this was a good thing, and felt relieved and grateful. But now that she had taken herself to Central America, she sensed that the threads that held her together might be loosening. She wasn't prepared for this letter barging in on her peaceful adventure, and amped up some bitterness. *So they sat on this information for how long? Like almost twenty years??* The metal frame of the cot dug into her thighs as she sat there with the mosquito netting draped around her shoulders like an ethereal shawl. Gradually, she could feel herself losing her vise grip on that roiling anger, and a layer of tears clouded her eyes. It's not like she wasn't still pissed. But seeping into the cracks was a warming gratitude, a sense of relief and of being cared for that was hard to discount. *Janet was trying to connect her with her birth mother. The same Janet who had ripped her away from family, and homeland, to live among aliens.*

In the center of the screen inside her mind, overlapping images now appeared: Her mother's letter, the Mayan woman questioning her identity, Martin and Rubi—whose story had so splintered her heart and unmasked the longing to know her own.

Gina carefully peeled herself off the cot frame and reached for her pack. She stepped out with her usual strong stride, but with no sense of direction that would normally go along with it. Julia, who was just then heading for the cold frame with a tray of seedlings, called out to her. "Where you going this time, girl-on-the-move?"

Shrugging her square shoulders, Gina answered her brightly this time. "No idea. Honestly!"

"Well, enjoy yourself when you get there."

"Yeah, I guess. Back soon."

She walked through the gate and left it yawning open. "Close the gate!" Julia yelled.

"Oh, sorry!"

"BUT not so hard. It's breakable!"

· · ·

The sun was surrendering into the arms of the trees and Gina absorbed herself with trying to capture this exceptional light inside her camera watching the beams play their way through the different shaped leaves and branches, yielding kaleidoscopes of white on the ground. She loved this time of day.

Thirty-eight captured images later, and twenty minutes down the road, she came upon vines slung over a small, tilted wooden sign. Pausing, she parted the tendrils with casual curiosity, looking for something readable. Her fingers only traced dust and wood splinters of a nameless color hovering between gray and brown. Then, after a moment's hesitation, Gina stepped into the yard and looked around.

A swing, dangling from a mahogany tree on a frayed rope, swayed like a pendulum at the end of its cycle, as if someone had only just jumped off and vanished. There were a few low-slung buildings around, two large barrack-type structures, and four smaller cabins. But where were the human sounds—voices, footsteps, clattering tin plates? Not even the wind rustled. The only sounds were flies buzzing, and the rhythmic tapping of the acorn woodpecker.

Gina spied what looked like a pump in a clearing off to the left. Her water bottle was nearly empty, and she wondered if potable water came out of this well. Should she chance it? She walked over to it, lifted the handle, and forced it down. The pump pierced the air with a screech. Further motion yielded a slightly softer sound, and she pumped out a strange melody with the rise and fall of its squeaky pitch until there was the thrill of gushing water.

"AHHH!"

She screamed, staggering under the weight of another body that had suddenly attached itself to her back. She pried away a pair of small, dirt-covered hands from her eyes, and unhooked the skinny legs clamped around her hips. When she flipped around, there was Rubi looking straight at her—actually smiling.

"I surprise you!" she said, clearly delighted with herself

"Yeah, I *guess*! I did not hear you coming at all. How'd you do that??"

"No zapatos" Rubi answered happily, looking down at her dirt-caked feet.

"Is this where you and Martin live? Where is everyone? Todos los otros?"

"You came to get me," was Rubi's response.

"What??"

"I know you came for us. I am happy. I tell Martin to get ready."

"Rubi, wait!!" But the child had already dashed off.

Gina considered running off herself— in the opposite direction.

But she had come this far, and something unseen had led her here, so she hurried after Rubi.

By the time she caught up with Rubi, her pink flip flops were back on, and she was cramming a t-shirt into her small, faded red backpack which seemed to hold everything of significance that was packable. Gina wondered if there were any family photos inside. She sat down on the little cot as Martin appeared in the doorway behind her.

"Rubi," she said quietly. "Are they nice to you and Martin here? Do you have enough food to eat? Are you going to school, not just working, working, working all the time?"

"Yes, yes, yes," piped up Martin, announcing his arrival. "Why are you here?"

"I don't know," Gina hesitated. "I was just taking a walk and my feet landed here."

Silence hung between them as before. Once again, she found it hard to tolerate that emptiness so she spoke up:

"I'm so glad to see you both, but I have no way to take care of you. Sometimes I wish I could, but I have no way. Are you safe here, Martin?"

"Yes. But I cannot be mama to Rubi. And the women here, they are so busy. Rubi is now old enough to help with the little ones, but in between, she is always looking for someone to be her mama. And last night she decided it must be you."

Gina took a deep, audible breath. "Rubi, come here a minute." She reached her arms toward her.

Rubi hesitated, then approached with two small steps. Gina scooped her up into her lap.

"I care so much about you and Martin," she said softly. "I will help you find whatever you need, but I must speak with Señora. And wherever I go, I will find a way to stay in touch with you."

Rubi looked at Gina steadily, without grasping what was being said. "But where are you going? I thought you work at the farm."

"Yes, yes, but just for now. I live in the U.S."

"I like to go to U.S."

"Oh, Rubi," Gina said, lightly tugging on the end of her braid. "I have no way to bring you there."

Martin came over to Rubi, and placed his hand lightly on her shoulder. He spoke a cascade of words in Spanish. Rubi nodded, then smudged some tears away.

"When are you leaving, Gina?" Martin asked solemnly.

"Oh, not yet. I'll be around awhile. I might go to Guatemala first." She was shocked that those never before spoken words had escaped her.

"Guatemala? Por que Guatemala?"

"I'm actually not sure." Gina looked from one to the other, as Rubi regarded her quietly.

"You looking for mama, tambien?"

"Well, I don't know." Gina, heart quivering with the shock of being seen. How could she be so transparent to a child who hardly knew her? Were her longings that obvious to everyone but herself? "Maybe I'll find her picture."

And in the quiet of the cabin, she told the two children her story, and where it might lead. They listened without interruption. Rubi leaned her cheek against Gina's shoulder.

Martin was the first to speak. "I wish we could come and help you with Spanish."

Gina smiled as she put her arm around Rubi.

"Thanks, Martin, but some trips you have to take by yourself, even if you don't speak the language very well. But I would like you to help me find Señora Giovanna, la directora, before I go back to the farm. Can you help me do that?" She unscrewed her water bottle, remembering her thirst.

"Don't drink that water!" yelled Rubi. "Sick!!" She grabbed her stomach and pretended to retch.

"Wow, thanks!! Just in time," said Gina.

A bit later, after speaking with the Señora, Gina headed back down the road with a feeling that some of the scattered pieces of herself were starting to flutter into place.

After making arrangements to extend her internship at the farm, she found the bus schedule and planned her trip to Guatemala City.

Thousands of miles away, Jase was slowly opening an envelope with a simple, puzzling sketch inside the folds of some fabric cinched together in the center which contained only a brief message: "From Gina. Explanation later, love in the meantime."

. . .

Gina awoke from a scant night's sleep. Her backpack was already stuffed with the few essentials she would need for her trip to Guatemala, and although it was probably too early to hike to the bus stop, she decided to leave then anyway.

As she emerged into the bright air of morning, her pack precariously hanging off one shoulder, she noticed there was no activity in the kitchen yet, and realized it must be really early. By now, of course, everyone on the farm knew about her impending adventure, which meant they also understood her adoption story. It was strange, but this new transparency was a lot more relaxing than all her evasion had ever been.

Suddenly her eye caught some movement, and she saw someone

coming around from the back of the kitchen. With a little squinting, she could just make out Julia's form bending toward a couple of children, hand outstretched, pointing in her direction.

Though the sun was in her eyes, Gina recognized the profile and slightly floppy running gait of Rubi and Martin, and she ran to meet them halfway.

Julia, who was walking behind the children, waved wildly.

"Hey, you weren't gonna try to sneak out of here without saying goodbye, were you? Well, even if you were, I'm here to inform you that is *not* allowed."

Gina laughed and scooped up the kids. Feeling their bones lock into hers was exactly what she needed.

"I wasn't sneaking. Really!"

"Yes, you were, but that's okay. 'Cuz we caught you, right Rubi?" Julia said.

Rubi grinned, and handed Gina a couple of pieces of paper covered with dusty little fingerprints.

"Thanks, you guys. I'll miss you this week, believe me!"

"Then we go, too!"

Gina put them both down on the ground and adjusted her pack which had slipped down to her elbow.

"Awww," she said. "Afraid not this time. But I'll see you very soon."

She tapped each child lightly on the cheek and gave Julia a hug. When she reached the gate, she could sense they were still watching her, and turned around halfway for one last wave.

45 minutes later, the rickety bus arrived that would take Gina to a larger bus station. She boarded with an unsteady heart and found two lumpy seats for herself. She gazed out the window, and then down at her hands, which were still clutching the pieces of paper. She opened the first one to find a drawing of her in her torn straw hat, holding a boy's hand on one side, a girl's on the other. No

words were written, or needed. Her heart was warmed completely.

The other piece was actually an envelope containing a return address: *Jase!* Expecting rejection, her pulse began to pound. She had ventured out on a slender branch of love in her last note to him, and here was his response. She swallowed a gulp of water before opening the envelope carefully. Seeing Jase's handwriting stirred her, but the message was brief:

> *When you are sketching the story of your life, don't let anyone else hold the pencil. (You heard this from me first.) Thinking of you, sometimes dreaming, too, Jase*

• • •

For a small moment, she could feel her heart give way.

Maybe I'm bigger than I thought I was. Maybe my mind can wonder. And maybe I really can hold many things at once. Without falling apart.

The bus jiggled along, shaking loose thoughts that had been glued together for a long time. Gina saw her life story, riddled with holes and contradictions. She could feel the heaviness of twenty years of effort to manage the pain by keeping it at bay. She had been working overtime to claim her life as if it had no history. But that struggle had wound her tight, keeping her small—and alone.

Now other images and feelings were merging into a free flowing current. Grief and gratitude, anger and love, two families, two cultures, questions answered and unanswered—all those faces and thoughts and rivers of emotion to make room for, without drowning. Gina was beginning to sense a curiosity, a daring, and a larger inner space to fill. She shifted in her seat and settled in for the ride.

PICK UP YOUR PEN

1. What do you imagine is ahead for Gina on her journey?

---

2. What either/or choices have you faced, and how have you resolved what felt like a conflict?

---

3. What has helped you to bring the different—sometimes warring—parts of yourself together?

---

4. What advice might you offer to another adoptee who has struggled with conflicting identities and emotions?

Creativity

Tools for Living, Sharing and
Making Sense of Things

I T IS SAID—AND WE KNOW IT TO BE A FACT—that the human brain is awesome. In the words of Indian author Ritu Ghatourey, "It functions 24 hours a day from the time we were born and only stops when you take an exam or fall in love."

On balance, this leaves lots of time for creative output.

For many transnational adoptees, a deep involvement in the arts has become an intrinsic part of the journey. Their paintings, photographs or sculptures hang in galleries and are displayed online. Their memoirs, stories and poetry are published. Their plays find their way to the stage. Their songs are sung at concerts and are accessible on YouTube. Transforming feeling and experience into art that is personally expressive offers a chance for others to resonate with what is presented and can be as deeply satisfying for artist as audience. From the moment we feel heard and seen—even if we ourselves are creator and first or only witness to the creation—healing begins to unfold. Art in all its forms provides this opportunity for everyone, privately or publicly, whether or not we are artistically gifted. Talent is not the point here. Expression is.

Any one of us can write a poem, make journal entries or sketches—not for evaluation and not necessarily for an audience. Extracting from our internal mix of feelings and experiences and then transforming that mix into color, shape, words, sound or movement—enhances the possibility for bringing the sometimes exiled parts of ourselves into the whole. Taking what seems invisible, banished or buried and making it real.

～

"It was through art that I began to have conversations with myself and tell my own story. I found that art made meaning for me and it recognized that my emotional experience mattered...The acknowledgement of my own loss and unknown has strengthened my love for inquiry and fueled my creativity." —TONYA FERRARO[53]

～

Adoptee artist Selena described how as a child she always struggled to understand her story. As she grew up, she found that making art helped her navigate the tangle of thoughts and emotions she experienced.

Here is a similar comment from an interviewee who also became a professional artist:

"Art has shaped me more than anything. My parents said I started creating my sculptures since I was four. They let me do what I wanted. I used whatever I could find: Toilet paper rolls, old deodorant containers...I always liked writing more than I liked being read to. And I loved to sit down and write books and illustrate them. They were always about people and animals being separated and coming back together, interestingly enough. I have boxes and boxes of these books, which I continued to make until I was 26."

～

The crafting of stories and works of art helped these adoptees make peace with the sense of loss that had existed from their earliest memories. Their creations which emerged from heart and imagination offered grief and longing a place of inclusion.

In the words of poet Lee Herrick, "I also understand now that when I write about adoption, I write about trauma. Yes, I write too about beauty. But this is about trauma. One has to dig for awhile through some tunnels before that light appears. But it does."[54]

SALVATION
by Lee Herrick

The blues means finding a song
in the abandonment, one you can sing
in the middle of the night
when you remember that your Korean name,
Kwang Soo Lee, means bright light,
something that can illuminate or shine, like tears,
little drops of liquefied God,
glistening down your brown face.[55]

Playwrite and actress Sun Mee Chomet explained that writing has helped her overcome confusion as well as to understand how to merge her own identity with the new history she is learning about as an adult.[56]

Vietnamese adoptee Jared Rehberg was inspired by the reunion of Operation Baby Lift adoptees in 2000 to write songs about his adoption experience. Like many others in that sweep of children that occurred as Saigon fell in 1975, he came to America without documentation that would give him a clue about his past.

INVISIBLE
song lyrics by Jared Rehberg

How am I different?
Are we really all the same?
Have you walked in my shoes?
Have you ever felt my pain?

I'm not invisible I'm right here
I'm not a child: you don't have to speak for me
I will be counted, you can count on me
I will be here, are you listening to me
To me...
Don't try and compare me
Or tell me how to feel
It's not about you,
It's about me.[57]

Adoption and creativity share elements of mystery and the unknown. These empty places can be painful, but they also offer opportunities. Adoptees use the arts to imagine places and people they have not seen or may never see.

"So what do you do if you don't know your own history?" asks writer Katie Hae Leo.

"You make it up, of course."

One adoptee, who is not a professional artist, spoke of making painting after painting as she imagined her home village in Russia and how this creative effort finally yielded some peace about unknowns that she had been seeking for a long time.

Artist and art therapist Sara Roizen writes:

"I...realized that not knowing my mother may actually fuel my constant desire to create. Without knowing my mother's face, I am free to create one for her....Symbolically, I reclaim my lost mother through the artistic process, evoking her through dialogues with my paintings. Art has given me a way to meet my mother metaphorically on the page or on the canvas...Those who know their biological family trees are assigned to a specific branch...Perhaps not knowing my family tree has freed me to paint my own...in various colors, shapes, types and settings."[58]

~

Adoptee Nari Baker created the exhibit, "Talking to Ghosts: Waiting in the River Between Worlds"[59] which included recordings of Korean adoptees speaking to their birth families who were not accessible, at the actual sites identified in their official documents and photographed for the exhibit. The project was born from Nari's own experience searching for and locating her birth mother in Korea, only to find that she refused to meet. This project helped her navigate her emotional turmoil.

~

"Artists are the gatekeepers of truth...My journey from mother to mother, home to home, drives my art....I started doing 'Talking Ghosts' by myself in Korea.

"The first part was figuring out how to talk to my family in the first person, what does that feel like...Then I decided to go to all these places from my records that I had never been to before. You could say I didn't really have the time, but it was more about I didn't really have the emotional capacity to go to all those places. I used this project as an excuse to do that...So I know that my story was one of 200,000. I eventually did seven other interviews with other adoptees in Korea, all site specific."

~

Creativity is a vital tool for self-expression, for exploring and empowering. It is available to everyone. Each of us has inborn ability and can channel feelings, perceptions, questions and experiences through the arts. Whether your creativity remains personal or shared, the value of your creative fire should not be underestimated.

To be sure, there are many extraordinary adoptee artists whose adoption experience has been grist for their creativity. A few of them are named here. I encourage you to explore their work to see if it resonates with you or inspires you to do your own. But most importantly—however you get there—let your unique experience, your perspective and your sometimes breaking, sometimes bursting heart speak for itself.

A SAMPLE LIST OF ADOPTEE ARTISTS

Nari Baker (artist), Keum Mee (writer), Gowe (rap artist), Dan Matthews (musician), Christina Seong (artist and designer), Jared Rehberg (songwriter), Trista Goldberg (film maker), Nicky Sa-eun Schildkraut (poet), Nicole Chung (writer/editor), Sun Mee Chomet (actor, dancer, playwright), Sara Tafere Barnes (painter), Katie Hae Leo (writer, performer, educator), Lynelle Long (photographer), Xhiv Bogart (painter).

PICK UP YOUR PEN:

Which avenue(s) of creative expression most appeals to you?

❑ Visual Art (Painting/Drawing/Photography/Filmmaking/

❑ Sculpting/Collage)

❑ Music (composing and/or performing)

❑ Writing (plays, articles, stories, blogs)

❑ Movement

❑ Public speaking/teaching/volunteering

Conclusion

Adoptees are survivors. Although often regarded by themselves and others as uniquely wounded, that is not nearly the whole story. Adoptees are also primed for strength, compassion and adaptability from the very beginning, where loss and radical change collided.

International adoption is a complex experience which can throw wrenches into your emotions, play tricks with your identity and rattle your sense of belonging. It involves an extra level of surrender to things beyond your control, beginning with the adoption itself and then most likely the lack of complete information about your history. At times, there may be waves of insecurity, anger and grief to ride as you come to accept life as it has been dealt.

Western culture teaches us to power through our emotional lives and the questions that plague us. The way of strength, we are told, is to keep busy and to "keep on keeping on." But in truth, snuffing out our personal narratives and strangling the accompanying emotions cannot be the way of strength. While avoiding difficult feelings can be sometimes be necessary and self-protective, as a lifelong habit it is a path to numbness.

Greater wisdom teaches us an alternative to stifling questions and feelings: That strength grows from giving ourselves permission to inquire and to make space for vulnerabilities, a true reservoir of power. Adoptees have compelling stories to tell. Voice them and claim who you are.

Research indicates that diversity enhances strength and endurance—in nature, in society, within committees and among coworkers. Even diversity within the human brain—openness to a variety of ideas and attitudes—is a source of creativity and flexible thinking which are strengthening. Moreover, if your background is multi-faceted—racially, culturally or nationally—chances are your understanding of the world can embrace complexities rather than simple, rigidly held ideas. The ability to embrace complexities helps us cope with life's inevitable challenges.

A broader perspective will always be an advantage. And just as mental flexibility is important to our well-being, there are many ways to revive it and to dislodge stuck energy. Physical movement and creative pursuits lift the spirits and help integrate feelings, thoughts and experience. Take a walk, dance, sing, paint, write. Remember to breathe.

And while you're at it, remember to laugh. There must be moments when you don't take the world or even your own life too seriously. Laughter and relaxation release tension. When the nervous system is calm, opportunities for new ways of thinking, feeling and healing abound.

Find the pace that works for you to take care of your emotional life. Feelings are fluid. They ebb and flow. They may be scary. They may be hard to express. But they are not wrong—they just are. Notice what and who are calming—and what and who are not.

Cultivate the former. Spend time in nature, listen to soothing music, create an oasis for yourself where you live. Find people you trust and open up to them. Consider finding a therapist specializing in adoption. What kind of support are you looking for, professional or kindred or both? Whatever you decide, it's a fact that no one will "get you" if you don't speak up.

Resilience flourishes when we take care of ourselves on all levels—rather than simply enduring or gutsing it out. Rooted in strength, adaptability and sheer life force, resilience is embedded in the babies who survived after being separated from birthmothers, whether abandoned in a box on a noisy street in Beijing or in a Mumbai orphanage where they suffered from lack of attention and nutrients. This resilience is born of a determination to survive, both before and after adoption.

As important as it is to name the tough feelings that grip us from time to time, it is equally vital to recognize that reservoir of strength that is yours, and then to feed and water it every day. All human beings are wounded and challenged and, yes, adoptees are wounded in unique ways. But just as unique is the inherent resilience, the strength and adaptability that grow out of this singular experience and multiple places of belonging. A resilience to depend on, to share and, truly, to celebrate.

∽

ALL THE WORLD IS FULL OF SUFFERING.

IT IS ALSO FULL OF OVERCOMING.

— HELEN KELLER

END NOTES

48 Aselefech Evans and Jenni Fang Lee conversation, YouTube, December 3, 2013 https://youtube/NDC3N1S1601.

49 "Twice Foreign," Shelise Gieseke, *Adoption Mosaic Magazine*, approx. 2011.

50 "International adoption: From a broken bond to an instant bond" by Michael Gerson, *Washington Post* opinion, August 27, 2010.

51 "Is the Left Launching an Attack on Evangelical Adoption?" by David French, *National Review*, April 25, 2013.

52 "Twice Foreign," Shelise Gieseke, *Adoption Mosaic Magazine*, approx. 2011.

53 Ferraro, Tonya, "Letters from an interdisciplinary artist: Illuminating Korean adoptee identity through mentors and metal," Graduate College Dissertations and Theses, Paper 5, University of Vermont, May 2014.

54 Poets on Adoption, poetsonadoption.blogspot.com, March 21, 2011.

55 Read the entire poem at www.fishousepoems.org

56 From "Perpetual Child: Adult Adoptee Anthology," Diane Rene Christian, Amanda H. L. Transue Woolston, editors, Createspace Independent Publishing Platform, November 22, 2013.

57 Excerpt from Jared Rehberg's song, "Invisible" www.jaredrehberg.virb.com

58 Sarah Roizen, "The Power of Art: Adoptee Artists/ The Artist's Path to Self: How does the adoption experience translate into art?" *Adoption Constellation Magazine*, July 25, 2011.

59 "Interpolated Spheres," works by Nari Baker, Darius Morrison and Christina Seong, interview by Minh Carrico, YouTube, Arts and Culture at Edmonds Community College, November 9, 2012.

Resources

WEBSITES, BLOGS AND GROUPS

Lost Daughters https://thelostdaughters.com

Light of Day Stories https://lightofdaystories.com

Spoonie Mama https://spoonie-mama.com

Harlow's Monkey https://harlows-monkey.com

Declassified Adoptee—Amanda Woolston
https://declassifiedadoptee.com

Red Thread Broken redthreadbroken.wordpress.com

Also-Known-As https://alsoknownas.org

Adopted and Fostered Adults of the African Diaspora

Vietnamese Adoptees – https://afaad.wordpress.com

Vietnamese Adoptees – https://www.facebook.com/
AdoptedVietnameseInternational

Colombian Adoptees – https://www.facebook.com/
AdoptedfromColombia

Ethiopian Adoptees of the Diaspora https://www.facebook.com/
ethiopianadopteesofthediaspora

Haitian Adoptees https://www.facebook.com/haitianadopteesgroup

Indian Adoptees https://www.facebook.com/lostsarees

Chinese Adoptees https://www.chineseadopteelinks.org

Intercountry Adoptees https://www.intercountryadopteevoices.com

Land of Gazillion Adoptees https://landofgazillionadoptees.com

Yoon's Blur https://yoonsblur.blogspot.ca

BOOKS

Coming Home to Self: The Adopted Child Grows Up by Nancy Verrier.

The Ghost of Sangjiu: A Memoir of Reconciliation by Soojung Jo.

Flip the Script: Adult Adoptee Anthology by Diane Christian.

All You Can Ever Know: A Memoir by Nicole Chung.

Parenting As Adoptees by Adam Chau and Kevin Ost-Vollmers.

For Black Girls Like Me by Mariama Lockington (middle grade).

This is The Journey by Alison Malee (poetry collection by an adoptee writer).

Adoption Healing...A Path to Recovery by Joe Soll.

ADOPTION DOCUMENTARY FILMS

Approved for Adoption by Jung Heinin.

Somewhere Between by Linda Goldstein Knowlton.

Operation Babylift by Tammy Nguyen Lee.

Las Hijas (The Daughters) by Maria Quiroga.

India: Calcutta Calling by Sasha Khokhat, one of the few films that focuses on the experience of an Indian adoptee.

First Person Plural by Deann Borshay Liem.

Crossing Chasms by Jennifer Arndt-Johns.

COUNSELING

The Center for Adoption Support and Education:
https://adoptionsupport.org
C.A.S.E. trains adoption-competent mental health professionals.

Crisis Text Line:
24/7 free, confidential support. Text HOME to 741741

ACKNOWLEDGEMENTS

THIS ALL BEGAN as a simple desire to hear direct unfiltered feedback from international adoptees about their experiences. It gradually evolved into a multi-layered project, thanks to the many people who helped push this initial collection of interviews through the keyhole into the outer world in book form. I am deeply grateful to each and every one.

First of all, I wish to express my great appreciation to all the adoptees I interviewed who shared their stories and, in the process, were willing to respond to challenging questions about sensitive subjects with thoughtfulness and candor. Thank you for the time and energy you gave to our conversations in the hope that what you have learned will light the way for other adoptees. I am honored by your trust and inspired by your resilience. I have learned so much from each of you.

Thank you as well to those whose words, wisdom or research appeared online and have been so richly meaningful: Shelise Gieseke, Mila Konomos, Shaaren Pine, Erica Gehringer, Kim Park Nelson and Amanda H.L. Transue Woolston among others. Your eloquence and forthrightness have broadened and deepened the contents of this book.

A special thank you to artists Stephen Johnson, Jared Rehberg, Addie Bara and Lee Herrick whose creativity has been so evocatively shaped by the experience of being an international adoptee. I am honored to have the unique expression of your imaginations within these pages.

Thank you to editor Deborah Mokma for your insightful contributions and to proofreader Sarah Bennett for your meticulous combing through the manuscript. To book designer Chris Molé for your steady guidance and design acumen, always offered with a generous dose of humor. I have also greatly appreciated the enthusiastic support of friends along the way whose interest never flagged.

And most especially my deep gratitude to Bob for the many hours reading every word, offering copious notes and excellent editorial clarity. All of your efforts, as well as your belief in the value of this endeavor, have been crucial in pushing it towards the finish line. Thank you for your unique blend of sparkling wit and invaluable wisdom—and, always, for the enduring joy of love and togetherness.

ABOUT THE AUTHOR

ANNE POLLACK has spent her career in human services and the arts. After earning her MSW from the University of Michigan, she worked in school, counseling and hospital settings. Following a chapter as a dancer, she trained in the Feldenkrais Method and worked in rehabilitation clinics with injured dancers and athletes. Years of experience as an adoptive parent led her to immerse herself in the challenges of international adoption by learning directly through interviews with adoptees themselves, as well as extensive research in adoptees' writings. Anne has lived throughout the US and Canada and currently resides in the Pacific Northwest with her family of humans and dogs.

Made in USA - Kendallville, IN
1220117_9780578679143
12.30.2020 1123